CULTURES OF THE WORLD
Cambodia

Cavendish
Square
New York

Published in 2017 by Cavendish Square Publishing, LLC
243 5th Avenue, Suite 136, New York, NY 10016
Copyright © 2017 by Cavendish Square Publishing, LLC

Third Edition

Library of Congress Cataloging-in-Publication Data

Names: Sheehan, Sean, 1951- author. | Cooke, Barbara, 1966- author. | Miller, Caitlyn, author.
Title: Cambodia / Sean Sheehan, Barbara Cooke, and Caitlyn Miller.
Description: New York : Cavendish Square Publishing, 2017. | Series: Cultures of the world | Includes bibliographical references and index.
Identifiers: LCCN 2016041875 (print) | LCCN 2016042198 (ebook) | ISBN 9781502622297 (library bound) | ISBN 9781502622303 (E-book)
Subjects: LCSH: Cambodia--Juvenile literature.
Classification: LCC DS554.3 .S54 2017 (print) | LCC DS554.3 (ebook) | DDC 959.6--dc23
LC record available at https://lccn.loc.gov/2016041875

Writers: Sean Sheehan and Barbara Cooke; Caitlyn Miller, third edition
Editorial Director, third edition: David McNamara
Editor, third edition: Kelly Spence
Associate Art Director, third edition: Amy Greenan
Designer, third edition: Jessica Nevins
Production Coordinator, third edition: Karol Szymczuk
Cover Picture Researcher: Angela Siegel
Picture Researcher, third edition: Jessica Nevins

PICTURE CREDITS

PRECEDING PAGE
A monk sits next to Angkor Wat.

Printed in the United States of America

CONTENTS

CAMBODIA TODAY

STANDING MORE THAN 600 FEET (183 METERS) TALL, THE ANCIENT temple of Angkor Wat towers above the surrounding Cambodian jungle. The temple complex has become a symbol of the country's rich history. Yet Angkor Wat has also become a driver of tourism, signifying the way that the ancient and the modern coexist in this Asian nation. Most Cambodians still farm and fish to earn a living; their way of life is in some ways remarkably similar to the people who built Angkor Wat hundreds of years ago. But in other ways, life in Cambodia is exceptionally modern, even for the farmers and fishermen who live in rural areas. Most people own at least one cell phone—many own a smartphone—and the economy of Cambodia is becoming ever more connected to the rest of the world. More than half a million Cambodians, 3 percent of the entire country's population, manufacture clothes that make their way to stores in the United States, Canada, and Europe. Globalization is increasingly changing life in Cambodia as the country opens up to the outside world. Still, Cambodians themselves remain connected to their cultural history and traditions.

Soldiers of the genocidal Khmer Rouge enter Phnom Penh.

Cambodia has a tumultuous modern history. Since gaining independence from France in 1953, the government of the country has changed many times. The most infamous period was undoubtedly under the Khmer Rouge—the genocidal regime led by Pol Pot—that killed up to two million Cambodians, a fifth of the entire population. Older Cambodians lived under this brutal dictatorship, and many lost family members and friends to the regime's crimes against humanity. The legacy of this time period is evident in the country: the economy is still recovering from the devastation of the time, and the trials (and appeals) of Khmer Rouge leaders are still taking place in the country's courts. But this terrible period is becoming less and less relevant to modern life in Cambodia with its extraordinarily young population. About 50 percent of Cambodians are under the age of twenty-four, meaning they were born more than a decade after the fall of the Khmer Rouge. Cambodians are looking to the future of their country rather than focusing on this dark period of its past.

Perhaps the greatest driver of change in Cambodia will be economic growth. Increasing levels of wealth will radically alter the way people live. In 2015, Cambodia's economy grew by 7 percent. This made it one of the top ten fastest-growing economies in the world. Cambodia has followed the model of China and prioritized manufacturing. The garment and footwear industry in particular has spurred huge levels of economic growth while also drawing criticism due to its poor working conditions and low wages. In every other country that has seen huge economic growth, the people's way of life has changed as well. People move from the country to cities; the number of people who farm decreases dramatically as technology reduces the need for labor; and the size of families shrinks. How exactly globalization and economic growth will shape the future of Cambodia remains to be seen, but it will almost certainly disrupt the current lifestyle of farmers that has lasted for millennia.

The current prime minister, Hun Sen, has ruled the country for more than thirty-five years. He took charge after Vietnamese forces removed the Khmer Rouge, and he has won every election since, although his critics dispute the fairness of these elections. As of 2016, he is sixty-four years old. Sooner or later, he will have to give up his leadership. Protests against his rule have been increasing in recent years, and the opposition party has gained increasing levels of support. If these efforts do not unseat him, Hun Sen himself has said he still step down in 2026 at the age of seventy-four. Whether he is defeated democratically by the opposition party, removed by protests, or eventually resigns in his old age, what is clear is a large political shift will soon come to Cambodia. It remains to be seen whether this political shift will finally tackle the problems of widespread corruption and low wages in the country or if another corrupt regime will take its place.

Despite modernization and the devastation of the Khmer Rouge, the culture of Cambodia remains resilient. The majority of Cambodians belong to the Khmer ethnic group. Their customs and ceremonies inform a number of the country's holidays and celebrations, but other thriving minorities also contribute to the cultural landscape of Cambodia. The dominant religion of Buddhism is integrally connected to most people's daily lives, and many festivals revolve around religious traditions. A small minority of Cambodians practice Islam as they have for centuries, and a growing number of Cambodians are adopting Christianity. These unique ethnicities and religions infuse present-day Cambodia with a rich cultural heritage.

While the Cambodia of today has its roots in ancient times, within the last thirty-five years the country has undergone a rapid transformation. As Cambodians begin to adopt new technologies, the country appears poised to achieve economic growth and the best quality of life in its history. However, Cambodians' pride in their heritage will undoubtedly preserve many elements of the nation's cultural traditions. As Cambodia moves forward, the future looks bright.

GEOGRAPHY

Houses built on stilts are necessary in some areas due to seasonal flooding.

CAMBODIA IS A SMALL COUNTRY located in Southeast Asia. It is bordered by Vietnam to the east, Laos to the north, and Thailand to the north and west. Its southern edge is situated on the Gulf of Thailand, a body of water that opens into the South China Sea, which is part of the Pacific Ocean.

With a land area of 68,152 square miles (176,515 square kilometers), Cambodia is just slightly larger than the state of Florida. It is smaller than all the countries that neighbor it. Most of the country is a flat plain that is prone to flooding during the rainy season, but mountains are also present near some borders. The powerful Mekong River and large lake of the Tonle Sap are the most prominent geographic features of the country. Their waters are integral to Cambodia's agriculture, and they serve as important routes for transportation by boat.

Cambodia's greatest width from east to west is 348 miles (560 kilometers). From north to south the farthest distance is 273 miles (440 km).

A so-called floating village on the Tonle Sap

LAND COVER

There has been a drastic change in Cambodia's land over the past three decades. While forests still cover about 60 percent of the country's total area, the amount of primary rain forest has plunged from approximately 73 percent in 1965 to just 3.1 percent in 2007. This is mostly due to years of illegal logging and rapid development. Since 2007, illegal logging and the clearing of vast tracts of land have continued, but there is no up-to-date information on how much of the rain forests remain. Water and swamps make up 3 percent, while 22.7 percent of the country's territory is arable, although not all of it is actually cultivated.

The Mekong River provides the focus for settled agriculture. Villages are spread out along both banks of the river and its tributaries as well as near the shores of the Tonle Sap. The various rivers also provide the main means of transportation for villagers and their produce.

THE CENTRAL PLAIN Cambodia's most important region is its central plain, where the regular flooding of the Mekong River and its tributaries replenishes the fertility of the soil. Over the centuries, people have used the regularity of the flooding as a way of irrigating their fields. The constant watering of the land makes it ideal for the cultivation of rice, which is the country's main source of food. The fertile land also allows for a variety of vegetables to be farmed. In addition, the rivers are a source of fish.

With a friendly climate that lacks extremes, Cambodia has favorable conditions for agriculture, which helps explain why the country has managed for centuries to escape the periodic famines that have afflicted other countries in this part of the world. The fertility of the alluvial plain also explains why the majority of Cambodians live in this part of the country.

Most of the central plain is gently rolling land; in the south, below the city of Phnom Penh, the plain becomes flatter.

Rice paddy fields require large amounts of water.

In Cambodia, the Mekong River is colloquially known as Tonle Thom, which translates to "Great River." It is the tenth-largest river (in volume) in the world. With a length of approximately 2,983 miles (4,800 km), it is Southeast Asia's most important waterway. At some places along its course, it widens to almost 2.5 miles (4 km).

The Mekong rises in Tibet and runs southward into Laos before entering Cambodia by a series of dramatic waterfalls. Once in the Cambodian floodplain, the river becomes navigable for the first time. The navigable portions, open to cargo ships, stretch from north of Phnom Penh to the river's delta in Vietnam. Before entering Cambodia, the Mekong has tremendous turbulence, forming some of the widest rapids in the world over a 6-mile (9.7 km) stretch in Laos. In Cambodia, there are also disruptive rapids just northeast of the capital. After flowing through Cambodia for about 315 miles (507 km), the Mekong splits into two branches south of Phnom Penh. The western branch becomes the Bassac River, while the eastern branch retains the name Mekong. It splits into numerous tributaries and forms a delta over an area of approximately 19,120 square miles (49,520 sq km) before emptying into the South China Sea in Vietnam.

The Mekong River is a highly trafficked waterway in Cambodia.

THE SURROUNDING MOUNTAINS

A number of mountain ranges ring the central plain. In the southwest of Cambodia lies a highland region formed by two mountain ranges. One is the granite Cardamom Mountains, which rise to a maximum height of 5,807 feet (1,770 m). The other range is the Elephant Mountains, which form a barrier between the lowlands of the central plain and the coastal region.

Isolated from the activity in the central plain, the southern coastal area remained largely undeveloped until several decades ago. It was not until the 1950s that a port town, Sihanoukville, was established. The only connecting railroad from Sihanoukville to the capital, Phnom Penh, was constructed between 1960 and 1969.

The northern border with Thailand is part of a sandstone escarpment that runs in an east-west direction and ranges in height from 1,640 to 2,297 feet (500 to 700 m). In the northeastern corner of the country is another mountainous region, reaching as high as 3,000 feet (900 m), formed by the eastern highlands. This is the most remote part of the country and home to indigenous ethnic groups that add to the richness of the country's culture.

The Cardamom Mountains have vast tracts of untouched rain forest.

TONLE SAP

The literal translation of the name of this natural reservoir is Great Lake. It was once just another tributary leading to the sea, but the continual silting up of the Mekong Delta turned the Tonle Sap into an inland lake. It is connected

DAMMING THE MEKONG

The Mekong River supports one of the world's most diverse fisheries, and more than sixty million people depend on it for food, water, transportation, and other daily needs. In 1995, the Mekong River Commission (MRC) was formed by an agreement between the governments of Cambodia, Laos, Thailand, and Vietnam. Through the MRC, these countries jointly manage water resources in the Mekong Basin and explore how to develop the economic potential of the river, alleviate poverty in the region, and protect and sustain the environment at the same time. Their wide-ranging programs focus efforts on several areas, including irrigation, drought and flood management, hydropower development, navigation, fishing, and tourism.

Over the past two decades, the MRC, together with the Asian Development Bank, has proposed more than one hundred dams for the purpose of generating electricity and flooding large areas for irrigation. While some dams have been built, with several more under development in Laos and Thailand, environmentalists continue to highlight the potential catastrophic human and ecological costs of such a plan. Finding a balance between harnessing the river's potential and safeguarding this natural resource has become a massive challenge.

The controversial Sesan 2 dam is still under construction.

to the Mekong at Phnom Penh by a 75-mile (120 km) channel of water known as the Tonle Sap River.

During the dry season, the Tonle Sap, the largest freshwater lake in Southeast Asia, is never more than 5 feet (1.5 m) deep. Between May and October—the wet season—the lower channels of the Mekong become so silted up that the floodwaters build up and cause the Mekong to rise as much as 45 feet (13 m) above its banks. Some of the surplus water backs up the Tonle Sap River and causes it to reverse its normal flow so that it runs northwest into the Tonle Sap.

During this wet period, the Tonle Sap's depth increases to as much as 40 to 45 feet (12 to 18 m), and from its former size of about 1,000 square miles (2,600 sq km) it can spread to an area of 4,020 square miles (10,400 sq km).

With the return of the dry season, water in the Mekong returns to its lower level and the Tonle Sap River reverses its flow, once again draining its waters into the Mekong. What is left behind, however, is the richest and most

Fishermen ply the waters of the Tonle Sap.

abundant area for freshwater fishing in the world. Estimates of fish yields from the Tonle Sap are in the region of 180,000 tons (164 million kilograms) a year.

CLIMATE

Cambodia has a tropical climate: temperatures are relatively high year-round. During April, the temperature in Phnom Penh averages 85.3 degrees Fahrenheit (29.6 degrees Celsius), with daily maximums of 89 to 104°F (32—40°C). December, the coldest month, sees an average temperature of 78.8°F (26°C).

Two monsoons dominate the annual climatic pattern. Between November and March, there is little rain from a dry, northeastern monsoon. During this period, in December and January, villagers harvest their rice. From May to October, a southwestern monsoon brings heavy rain and strong winds. The

The streets of Phnom Penh often flood in heavy rains.

rain often falls during the afternoon in a series of intermittent bursts. The southwestern monsoon produces about three-quarters of the country's total annual rainfall.

In the central plain, nearly 72 inches (1.8 m) of rain falls during the six months of the southwestern monsoon. The eastern coast of the United States, by comparison, receives about 48 inches (1.2 m) over twelve months. In between these two periods, during April and May, the weather is a mixture of the two, even though April is also the hottest month of the year.

April is, for the most part, the most uncomfortable month for Cambodians; it is very humid, and there are only a few light showers to ease the heat. Toward the end of the month, however, the rainy monsoon approaches and the first rains begin to fall. This change in weather is marked with festive celebrations, most notably the Khmer New Year, which is the biggest holiday in Cambodia.

WILDLIFE

The flora of the central lowland region is governed by the importance of agriculture. Rice fields are the most characteristic feature of the landscape, alongside fields of other crops, such as tobacco and corn. In the north, where mountains predominate, evergreen forests are found. In the southwest, there are tracts of primary forest and teak trees.

Teak is a common tree in Cambodia, although it is not native to the country. It was introduced toward the end of the seventeenth century. Teak is an important and valuable source of water-resistant timber. Being extremely heavy, teak will sink in water unless it has been completely dried, so the tree's bark is removed and the tree is left to dry for two years before it is cut down. Pine trees grow at higher elevations in the southwest. Along the 273-mile (440 km) coastline, mangrove forests face the Gulf of Thailand, while along the inland rivers, lotuses are common. The lotus of Cambodia, also found in China and India, is considered sacred and is traditionally associated with the Buddha.

Large wild animals that are becoming increasingly rare in most parts of the world continue to roam the Cambodian countryside. Elephants, leopards,

The Preah Vihear temple, located on the mountainous Cambodian-Thai border, is claimed by both Cambodia and Thailand. There have been numerous border clashes over the temple—most recently in 2008.

and wild oxen are still present in some areas. Before war erupted in the 1970s, affluent game hunters from around the world regarded Cambodia as prime territory for shooting wild animals. However, years of civil war and the United States' bombing in parts of Cambodia during the Vietnam War resulted in large-scale environmental damage, which drastically decreased the wildlife population. Poaching in Cambodia has also contributed to this decline.

The most unusual animal in Cambodia was the kouprey, a wild forest ox that was identified only in 1939 and was designated as the country's national animal in 1960. The kouprey is most likely extinct. Some unconfirmed sightings provide hope that a small number still survive in remote parts of the country. However, following the civil war, land mines and hunting remain a threat to any that remain.

Cambodia has a rich and diverse birdlife, including elegant birds such as pelicans, herons, egrets, and cranes, and colorful birds such as tropical parrots and kingfishers. Cormorants, pheasants, and grouse are also common. Fish-eating water fowl are especially common around the Tonle Sap because of the quantities of fish brought in when flooding occurs.

The sun bear is indigenous to parts of Cambodia.

Phnom Penh, the capital, is Cambodia's largest city, with an estimated 1.5 million people. It is situated at the confluence of the Mekong, Bassac, and Tonle Sap Rivers in the central plain. Phnom Penh was founded in 1434 to succeed Angkor Thom as the capital but was abandoned several times, when different kings shifted the capital to Lovek. It was reestablished in 1865. Despite being 180 miles (290 km)

from the sea, it is a major port, linked to the South China Sea via the Mekong River.

Other urban centers include Battambang (147,000 people) and Sihanoukville, the former Kampong Som (250,000).

INTERNET LINKS

www.britannica.com/place/Cambodia
Encyclopedia Britannica provides information about Cambodia's terrain, climate, animal and plant life, and seasonal flooding.

www.cia.gov/library/publications/the-world-factbook/geos/print_cb.html
The CIA's *World Factbook* contains information about the geography of Cambodia as well as pictures of the country.

www.tourismcambodia.com/about-cambodia/geography.htm
A site established by the Cambodia Ministry of Tourism, Tourism Cambodia gives an in-depth look at Cambodian geography.

Pol Pot, the Khmer Rouge's reclusive leader

2

THE FIRST EVIDENCE OF HUMAN habitation in Cambodia goes back at least seven thousand years from today to the Stone Age. Archaeologists have found stone tools that hunter-gatherers made in Cambodia from this time. Bronze Age artifacts have also been unearthed from a number of sites across the country. Unlike North America or Europe, there are remarkable similarities between life thousands of years ago in Cambodia and life there today. Fish and rice were the main food source, as they are now, and the language was likely even an early form of Khmer (which is spoken today) or a closely related language.

In the centuries before and after the beginning of the Common Era, a process of acculturation took place in Cambodia. Contact with traders and envoys from India led to a cultural shift in Cambodia and other countries in Southeast Asia. The Hindu religion was adopted, and irrigation and theories of governance were also borrowed from the Indian visitors. While this process was (and is) called "Indianization," Cambodia

Buddhist art predates the arrival of Hinduism in Cambodia.

retained many aspects of its own culture. It did not completely assimilate, and India never exercised political control over the region.

THE FIRST KINGDOM

A Cambodian legend links the kingdom of Funan with India through an Indian Brahmin priest called Kaundinya. The Brahmin possessed the magical power to force anyone he chose into marrying him. He picked Soma, the daughter of the Lord of the Soil (a ruler of the Mekong Delta). Their marriage led to the founding of the Lunar Dynasty of Funan. As a wedding present, the Lord of the Soil obligingly drank the flooding waters of the Mekong, thereby enlarging their territory and enabling the people to cultivate the land.

The legend is testimony to the importance of Indian influence in the development of the Funan kingdom. It was established around the second or third century CE by migrants from southern China. Its importance resulted from its strategic position in the trade route between India and China. Since merchant ships liked to keep the coast in sight as they turned to the north around the Mekong Delta, any coastal settlement was bound to offer itself as a stopping place. Funan's major port was in what is now southern Vietnam, but the kingdom included most of modern Cambodia.

THE KHMER EMPIRE

In the sixth century the Funan kingdom splintered, and a period of instability followed. In the eighth century, present-day Cambodia was taken over by Java (now part of Indonesia).

The first ruler of the Khmer Empire was Jayavarman II. He was of Javanese origin, but his importance is due to his assertion of independence from Java. Equally significant was his declaration of god-given powers. He proclaimed himself more than a king—he was a god-king, allied to Shiva, one of the three rulers of the Hindu gods. It was during the reign of his nephew, Indravarman (who ruled between 877 and 889), that large-scale irrigation of the Mekong River began. As the system of irrigation was developed and extended, a more settled agricultural society was created. The resulting stability led to an increase both in population and in the power of the ruling dynasty. Under the rule of Yasovarman (889—900) the capital was moved to the area around Angkor. This was the first step in what would become an astonishing flowering of artistic excellence, expressed in architecture and sculpture, that continues to fascinate the world.

Apart from a brief period in the tenth century, Angkor remained the political and cultural heart of Cambodia until the middle of the fifteenth century. The interruption was caused by an invasion from Vietnam, which resulted in the sacking of Angkor. When Khmer rule was restored by

Angkor Thom

Jayavarman VII (1181—1218), there was a need to rebuild Angkor. What followed was an ambitious and impressive program of reconstruction, and the major site of Angkor Thom came into being.

THE END OF THE KHMER EMPIRE

Historians offer differing explanations for the demise of the Khmer Empire. But all agree that the growing hostility of neighboring Thailand was a prime factor. Thai rulers made constant attempts to destabilize their Angkorian rivals in an attempt to extend their own territory. Each attempted invasion from Thailand disrupted the elaborate irrigation system on which Angkorian society depended. The need to militarize the country also slowed down—and eventually stopped—the upkeep of the temples and the building of new ones. The temples existed to sanctify the rule of the god-kings. When they fell into a state of disrepair, it revealed the weakening hold of the rulers over their people.

Cambodia's history as a French colony is still visible in the architecture of some buildings.

By the middle of the fifteenth century, Angkor had fallen to Thailand. The rulers deserted their capital and retreated to an area around Phnom Penh. For the next century and a half, an ongoing war was fought between the Thais and Khmers. The Thais were pushed back out of the country, but in 1594 they returned in force and Angkor was again occupied.

Until the arrival of the French, Cambodia was ruled by various kings. The kings were continually fighting off challenges to their power from within their own royal families. Alliances were made with either Thailand or Vietnam to gain military support, and in return, Thais and Vietnamese were allowed to settle in the respective border regions. During this period, the Vietnamese began to populate what is now the southern region of Vietnam, an area that was once part of Cambodia.

FRENCH COLONIZATION

By the 1860s, Cambodia was in imminent danger of being completely absorbed by either Thai or Vietnamese rule. Both countries were able to invade Cambodia at will; only their own rivalry kept Cambodia intact. As a result, in 1863 the French had little difficulty persuading King Norodom to sign a treaty placing the kingdom under French protection.

Cambodia was incorporated into a Union of Indochina, governed by a resident-general based in Hanoi. French administrators were introduced. Slavery was abolished, and modern schools were built. The Khmer elite received a French education and were introduced to French culture. To maintain order and dampen any threat of nationalist sentiment, the French continued to support the monarchy.

In the early 1940s, Japan seized de facto control of Cambodia. Cambodia was now part of Japan's "Greater East Asia Co-prosperity Sphere." The provinces of Battambang and Siem Reap were ceded to Thailand, while the French were allowed to retain nominal control in the rest of the country. After Japan's surrender, which brought World War II to an end, the two northwestern provinces were returned by Thailand, and Cambodia was recognized as an autonomous kingdom within the French Union.

King Sihanouk

By then, a growing sense of Cambodian nationalism was brewing. In 1953, Norodom Sihanouk, who had been crowned king in 1941, proclaimed his country's independence from France. He began a crusade to gather international support, and before the end of 1954 the French recognized that Cambodia was no longer one of their colonies.

THE KINGDOM OF CAMBODIA

The first two decades of independence were a difficult time for Cambodia. Sihanouk had to contend with domestic threats to his rule, and in 1955 he abdicated the throne in order to establish his own political party. A parliament had been created after independence, so the monarchy could no longer exercise absolute rule. Sihanouk's party easily won control of the parliament.

In the 1960s, Cambodia's neighbor Vietnam became increasingly embroiled in a civil war that also involved the United States. At first Sihanouk proclaimed his country's neutrality, but neutrality became increasingly more difficult. By 1965, Sihanouk felt that the United States was conspiring against him because of his refusal to support South Vietnam in its war against North Vietnam. Cambodia turned instead to North Vietnam and allowed the Viet Cong to use its territory as a base in its war against the Americans.

In 1969, the United States began a secret bombing campaign of suspected Viet Cong bases in Cambodia. The bombing continued for four years and increased in scope until vast areas in the east of the country were being systematically carpet bombed by US B-52s. In March 1970, Sihanouk was deposed by Lon Nol, one of his generals, with US support, and the country was invaded by US and South Vietnamese troops.

THE RISE OF THE KHMER ROUGE

Cambodia's new ruler, Lon Nol, presided over an increasingly corrupt administration. Guerrilla armies withdrew from the towns and began gaining influence over the countryside. Hundreds of thousands of people died in the fighting that engulfed the country. Even military and financial support from the United States could not stem the tide of civil war. In April 1975, the capital, Phnom Penh, flooded by well over one million refugees, fell to the Khmer Rouge, who became the new rulers of Cambodia.

The Khmer Rouge, with Pol Pot as its leader, believed that Cambodia's problems were the result of its colonial history. It felt that the country should return to a primitive, self-sufficient agricultural state. Returning to the past—to "Year Zero"—meant abolishing money, schools, twentieth-century technology, and newspapers. The sanctity of the family unit and the establishment of homes in a town or city were regarded as antirevolutionary. This meant emptying cities of their entire population (Phnom Penh became a ghost town), breaking up families, and imposing collective agriculture. All

these were accomplished under a rule of extreme harshness and brutality that resulted in the deaths of at least one million civilians. People died from lack of food or from disease. Doctors, like teachers and other middle-class professionals, were executed for being antirevolutionary, and hospitals were closed down. Many others died from overwork.

Photographs of victims of the Khmer Rouge

THE CAMBODIAN-VIETNAMESE WAR

At the end of 1978, the Vietnamese army poured across the border and swiftly brought to an end the rule of Pol Pot and the Khmer Rouge. Vietnam had invaded Cambodia to protect its western territory from hostile raids by the Khmer Rouge. Although Vietnam had liberated Cambodia from tyranny, the rest of the world was reluctant to recognize the puppet government installed in Phnom Penh. American hostility to communist Vietnam played a large part in ensuring that Pol Pot's Democratic Kampuchea kept its seat at the United Nations.

Cambodians suffered the aftermath of a disrupted rice harvest brought about by the Vietnamese invasion, and many died. Only an international famine relief program rescued the country from a devastating famine.

In 1998, Pol Pot, the man who once controlled Cambodia, was being held under house arrest by the remnants of the Khmer Rouge. Having been forced out of power decades earlier, the Khmer Rouge was reduced to a small group of guerrilla fighters hiding along the border with Thailand. On April 15, 1998, the radio station Voice of America broadcast that Pol Pot was to be turned over to stand trial for his crimes after being betrayed by his own movement. But he died that very same night. The commander holding him claimed it was from natural causes; however, the time of his death led to speculation that he had committed suicide or been killed. His body was cremated, so there will never be a definitive answer to this question. What is clear, though, is Pol Pot escaped justice and was never held accountable for his crimes.

Khmer Rouge leader Kaing Guek Eav was sentenced to thirty-five years' imprisonment.

Other leaders of the Khmer Rouge cannot say the same. The UN and the government of Cambodia set up the Khmer Rouge Tribunal to seek justice for victims of the genocidal regime. Thus far, three leaders of the Khmer Rouge have been sentenced to life imprisonment for genocide, war crimes, and crimes against humanity. The two most recent verdicts were returned in 2014, more than thirty years after the Khmer Rouge was driven out of power by Vietnamese forces. The verdicts of the tribunal sent a clear message that the victims of the Khmer Rouge have not been forgotten and those guilty of terrible crimes against humanity will never be safe from justice no matter how much time has passed.

By 1985, the Vietnamese had forced the Khmer Rouge into Thailand. From there Pol Pot's army continued to plague the country by mounting guerrilla attacks and planting thousands of land mines that continue to wreck the lives of Cambodians.

Vietnam's intervention in Cambodia lasted for nearly eleven years. It ended when Mikhail Gorbachev, leader of the Soviet Union, began to press for withdrawal. By the end of 1989, the last Vietnamese troops had left Cambodia.

A PLAN FOR PEACE

An internationally sponsored peace agreement was signed in Paris in 1991. Early the following year, the United Nations Transitional Authority in Cambodia (UNTAC) arrived to pave the way for democratic elections. The signatories to the peace plan included representatives from most of the political groups that had held or sought power in Cambodia over the previous two decades. A new coalition government emerged, dedicated to building a new future. The Khmer Rouge signed the peace treaty but then failed to honor its terms and boycotted the elections. Factional fighting led to Pol Pot's capture by a Khmer Rouge commander and a show trial in 1997. He died a year later. By the end of 1999 most of the remaining leaders had either surrendered or were caught, and the Khmer Rouge came to an end.

In the next chapter we will take a closer look at the history of Cambodia since the peace agreement of 1991. These early years of the new incarnation of the Kingdom of Cambodia were critical in shaping the current system of government.

The United States dropped more than half a million tons (453,592 metric tons) of bombs on Cambodia and caused the death of about the same number of civilians and soldiers. The bombing was finally stopped by the US Congress in August 1973.

INTERNET LINKS

www.bbc.com/news/world-asia-pacific-13006828
The BBC provides a timeline of Cambodian history from 1941 (the occupation of Cambodia by the Japanese) to present day.

www.cambodiatribunal.org/history/cambodian-history/khmer-rouge-history
This site includes a history of the rise and fall of the Khmer Rouge in Cambodia.

www.pbs.org/pov/enemies/photo-gallery-timeline-cambodia-khmer-rouge
PBS provides a timeline of the Khmer Rouge and the trials of its high-ranking officials. Videos and pictures are included.

GOVERNMENT

The National Assembly of Cambodia

3

THE STRUCTURE OF CAMBODIA'S government is democratic. Yet one man, Hun Sen, has been the prime minister of Cambodia for more than thirty years, and this fact betrays the less-than-democratic nature of Cambodia's current government. Hun Sen's tenure as prime minister has not been peaceful. In addition to a 1993 coup against his co-prime minister, Norodom Ranariddh, Hun Sen also used violent repression against peaceful protestors in 2014.

Over the years, many journalists and opposition leaders have died violent deaths that were not thoroughly investigated by the government. As a result, many claim Hun Sen himself was behind the deaths of numerous political opponents and critics of his rule. These facts have led many groups, such as Human Rights Watch and Amnesty International, to liken him to a dictator rather than a democratically elected leader.

We will first look at the formation of Cambodia's current government before turning to the structure of the government under the constitution. But it is important to remember that the actual state of the current Cambodian government is very different from the democratic one that the constitution outlines. International organizations consider Cambodia to be highly corrupt with a very restricted press.

THE FOUNDATION OF THE GOVERNMENT

In 1993, the United Nations mounted what was then the biggest (22,000 troops) and most expensive ($1.6 billion) peace operation in its history. The purpose was to manage a general election in Cambodia, a country that had been torn apart by more than twenty years of civil war.

The United Nations managed to register 4.2 million voters, established over 1,400 polling stations, and brought back 360,000 refugees who had been living in camps in Thailand. Some 50,000 Cambodians were trained by the United Nations to help facilitate the elections. Another 1,400 officials were recruited from other countries for two weeks to monitor the process.

Candidates from twenty parties registered for election. However, the four warring factions that signed the Paris Peace Agreement in 1991 formed the main political parties. The Khmer Rouge became the Party of Democratic Kampuchea (PDK). The Vietnamese-backed government that ran Cambodia following Vietnam's invasion in 1978 became the Cambodian People's Party (CPP). A royalist group headed by Prince Norodom Sihanouk's son Norodom Ranariddh reverted to its old name, the National United Front for an Independent, Neutral, Peaceful, and Cooperative Cambodia (FUNCINPEC), while a noncommunist group headed by Son Sann split into the Buddhist

His real name was Saloth Sar, but he later took the name Pol Pot and was often simply referred to as "Brother Number One" for his leading role in the Khmer Rouge. Born into a peasant family in 1925, he was not academically outstanding. Nevertheless, he won a scholarship to study in Paris. It was there that he further developed his communist ideas, which had first taken shape while he was in school in Phnom Penh. His interest in politics eventually lost him his scholarship, and he returned to Cambodia in its early years of independence. In 1963, he fled into the countryside, where he rose through the ranks of the Communist Party of Kampuchea to become its secretary-general. He trained in guerrilla tactics, and by the time Khmer Rouge forces took over the capital in 1975, he was the undisputed leader.

For the vast majority of Cambodians, so many of whom suffered terribly under his regime, Pol Pot remained a shadowy figure. He was never the subject of a personality cult, and his name meant nothing to the millions of people who endured the return to "Year Zero." Pol Pot was a recluse. When his troops took the capital in 1975, he did not appear in any of the victory parades that followed. He entered the city quietly, after it had been emptied of people. Very few foreigners had ever seen him, and only a handful had ever spoken to him.

Pol Pot died in 1998. He is thought to have been about seventy-two years old. However, the legacy of war and terror remains as thousands of land mines laid by his troops continue to maim civilians. During the 1980s, a National Hate Day was held every May 20, providing an opportunity for Cambodians to renounce everything Pol Pot stood for. Gatherings of civilians took place at village cemeteries and sites associated with former atrocities, and the crimes of the past were remembered in an attempt to come to terms with them.

Liberal Democratic Party (BLDP) and the Liberal Democratic Party (LDP).

The PDK, or Khmer Rouge, having gained some legitimacy by signing the Paris Peace Agreement, then denounced the elections and threatened to disrupt them. Pessimists predicted that the elections would be rendered meaningless by guerrilla tactics from dissident groups. During the election in May 1993, some Cambodians were killed. Nevertheless, by the time the polls closed, a very large percentage of the electorate (some 90 percent) had exercised its hard-won right to vote.

THE 1993 ELECTIONS

The elections were considered a success by international observers. As expected, no one party emerged a clear victor. The three parties that won the most seats in the 120-member National Assembly were FUNCINPEC (58 seats), the CPP (51 seats), and the BLDP (10 seats). These parties, though representing different policies and ideologies, were forced into an alliance to form a government. Votes accorded to the CPP showed that, despite being installed by the Vietnamese military, the party had saved the country from Pol Pot. The votes given to FUNCINPEC reflected the strong anti-Vietnam and anticommunist sentiment in the country. In October 1993, Prince Ranariddh of FUNCINPEC was installed as first prime minister, with Hun Sen of the CPP as second prime minister.

THE STRUGGLE TO REBUILD

Prince Norodom Ranariddh

Intellectuals and professionals were once purged from Cambodia. Now, the Royal University of Phnom Penh has more than twelve thousand students.

When the United Nations left Cambodia after the 1993 elections, an immediate problem emerged over who would maintain law and order. It would be some time before the newly unified Cambodian army could function effectively. Creating an army and police force free of corruption was another challenge facing the government.

Even more fundamental was the task of creating a government. Under the Khmer Rouge regime, there was a systematic destruction of intellectuals and professionals. Those who managed to escape death fled the country. Cambodia faced a dire shortage of educated and middle-class professionals able to put together and run a government.

There was also the problem of the absence of a legal framework or an independent judiciary. A twenty-year interruption in normal civil life creates enormous problems for any government. Aspects of life that most countries take for granted, like going to court when there is a dispute over the legality of an act or business contract, had to be brought into existence in a country that had been forced to manage without them.

Despite the recent history of Cambodia, the country has managed to create a remarkably open society in many respects. Debates in the National Assembly are televised live, and there are often open discussions about the problems facing the country.

THE COUP OF 1997

Within months of forming a government, Ranariddh ordered the country's army to mount a series of offensives against the Khmer Rouge guerrillas. Thousands of guerrillas turned in their arms and defected to the government.

By 1997, Ranariddh and Hun Sen were in a fierce battle for control of the government as they both tried to win the support of Khmer Rouge defectors. Fighting broke out between their supporters. Fearing that Ranariddh's soldiers would welcome any remaining Khmer Rouge guerrillas into their ranks, Hun Sen staged a bloody coup, overthrowing Ranariddh on July 7, 1997. Numerous opposition figures were killed, and Ranariddh fled the country.

Prime Minister Hun Sen

THE CONSTITUTION

Cambodia's present constitution was adopted in September 1993. Cambodia is a representative democracy under a constitutional monarchy. The main provisions of the constitution are:

THE KING The king is the head of state and supreme commander of the Khmer Royal Armed Forces. The king appoints the prime minister and the cabinet and holds office for life.

In the event of the king's death, the Royal Council of the Throne (composed of the president of the National Assembly, the prime minister, the supreme patriarchs of Cambodia's two main Buddhist groups, and the first and second vice chairmen of the National Assembly) must select a new king from among the descendants of three royal lines within seven days.

King Norodom Sihamoni

NATIONAL ASSEMBLY Legislative power lies with the National Assembly, which has at least 120 members. Members are elected to a term of five years by universal adult suffrage. Only Cambodian citizens by birth who are over the age of twenty-five can run for election to the National Assembly.

SENATE The Senate was created in 1999 by a constitutional amendment. It is composed of sixty-one senators. Fifty-seven are elected by local parliamentarians and commune councils from Cambodia's twenty-four provinces. Two are chosen by the king, and two are elected by the National Assembly. The Senate has little real power under the constitution—it primarily functions in an advisory role.

CABINET The cabinet is led by a prime minister and assisted by deputy prime ministers. Other members of the cabinet are state ministers, ministers, and state secretaries. The prime minister appoints the members of the cabinet, who must be representatives in the National Assembly or members of parties represented in the National Assembly.

THE CONSTITUTION COUNCIL The Constitution Council interprets the constitution and laws passed by the National Assembly. The council consists of nine members with a nine-year mandate. One-third of the members are appointed by the king, three elected by the National Assembly, and three appointed by the Supreme Council of the Magistracy.

THE 2013 ELECTION: PROTESTS AND VIOLENCE

The most recent general election in Cambodia was in 2013. Officially, Hun Sen's CCP won the most votes with 48.83 percent of the popular vote. The major opposition party, the Cambodia National Rescue Party, won 44.46 percent of the vote. This gave the CCP a majority in the National Assembly. But opposition leaders accused the CPP of manipulating the election results, and international organizations, as well as the government of the United States, called for an investigation into the matter. The government of Cambodia, led by the CPP, refused to investigate these claims. In response, protests were staged across the country. Over time, anger against the government spread, and garment factory workers began to strike to demand a higher minimum wage. The government demanded the protests and strikes end. When they did not, a police crackdown dispersed crowds of protesters and striking workers across the country. Four workers were killed and many more injured by gunshots during the crackdown—police reportedly fired into a crowd of people. Other activists were arrested by authorities. After the crackdown, the government granted some concessions: the minimum wage was increased slightly for some groups of workers, and the opposition party negotiated some political reforms. Yet overall, no substantial reforms were made, and the Cambodian government's strict control continues to impede freedom of speech.

INTERNET LINKS

www.economist.com/topics/cambodia
The *Economist*'s collection of published stories about Cambodia offers a glimpse of recent political events in the country.

www.hrw.org/asia/cambodia
This website gives a short description of human rights in Cambodia with a link to Human Rights Watch's yearly report on the country and recent articles about Cambodia.

www.voacambodia.com/p/6019.html
Voice of America Cambodia has a section on domestic news containing many stories related to politics.

A constitutional amendment in 2014 put measures in place to guarantee the independence of the National Election Committee from any political party.

ECONOMY

Workers in one of Cambodia's many garment factories

CAMBODIA REMAINS ONE OF THE poorest countries in the world after the disastrous reign of the Khmer Rouge and limited development under the North Vietnamese–backed government of the 1980s. Rapid economic growth in recent years has significantly decreased poverty in Cambodia. In 2004, 54 percent of Cambodians lived in poverty. In 2012, just 17.7 percent of the population lived in poverty. Few countries in the world have achieved such a significant reduction in poverty in such a short amount of time. While many challenges still face the economy of Cambodia, economic growth remains strong, and at the beginning of 2016, the World Bank reclassified Cambodia as a lower middle-income country instead of a low-income country.

4

In September 1994, oil and natural gas were discovered by a British oil company about 124 miles (200 km) southwest of Sihanoukville.

THE IMPACT OF THE KHMER ROUGE

The economic problems facing Cambodia in the 1990s were enormous. During the decades of civil war, few businesses paid taxes. At one stage in the early 1990s, the inflation rate was 90 percent a month, and the country's unit of currency, the riel, was almost worthless.

After the election of 1993, the government that emerged had to rebuild a viable economy from scratch. The new administration took immediate steps to bolster the country's weak economy: corporate taxes were collected and all commercial enterprises were required to maintain a record of their financial transactions. The currency has now been stabilized, and inflation has been brought under control.

When the Khmer Rouge set out to return the country to "Year Zero," they envisioned a pre-industrial-age society in which money had no place. This policy devastated the Cambodian economy, which had already been weakened by years of civil war.

After the Vietnamese overthrew the Khmer Rouge, Western nations imposed a trade-and-aid embargo, hampering Vietnamese attempts to rebuild a working economy. Since the 1990s, foreign aid has reached Cambodia, with many foreign companies eager to invest in the country.

AGRICULTURE

Nearly half of Cambodians make a living from agriculture. However, rice yields in Cambodia are among the lowest in the world, partly due to the lack of fertilizer, which most farmers cannot afford to purchase.

A strain of rice known as floating rice is unique to Cambodia. The rice alters its rate of growth in response to the rise of floodwaters. The grain heads remain above the water at all times, hence the term "floating rice."

The country's food supply was severely damaged by over two decades of militarization. In the late 1960s, the country was able to export half a million tons (454,000 t) of rice every year. During the 1980s and 1990s, Cambodia had difficulty feeding its population and needed the United Nations to make up for the food shortage. Today Cambodia produces more than enough food to satisfy domestic consumption, but one-third of the population still has difficulty obtaining the minimum daily food requirements due to inefficient distribution systems.

The next most important crop is corn, followed by cash crops—crops grown for income. The principal cash crop is rubber. There are 983,500 acres (389,000 hectares) of rubber trees in Cambodia. But in recent years the price of rubber has plummeted, leading to uncertainty in the industry. A ton of rubber used to fetch $4,500 in 2011. Yet as of the middle of 2016, it is valued at less than $1,600. This sharp drop in price is due to increased production in the main rubber-producing countries of Thailand, Indonesia, and Malaysia. It has decreased the profitability of producing rubber in Cambodia as well. Other cash crops include cotton, tobacco, pepper, and sugar palms.

Apart from rice, fishing is the most important source of food for most Cambodians. The majority of villages exist close to a waterway or have large ponds to provide fish. Around 50 percent of all fish caught and consumed is taken from Tonle Sap Lake. The fishing season lasts from October to February. However, the number of fish in Tonle Sap has been decreasing in recent years as overfishing and the destruction of the surrounding environment deplete fish stocks.

MINING

There are no known significant deposits of minerals in Cambodia. Limited deposits of iron ore, limestone, kaolin, tin, bauxite, and silver have been found but are not exploited commercially.

Since 1991, some small-scale gold mining has taken place in the province of Kampong Cham. Deposits of phosphates are located in the southern province of Kampot and are processed in plants situated in Battambang and Kampot for use as fertilizers. There is rich potential for oil and natural gas extraction in Cambodia. In the early 1990s, foreign companies began competing to drill both onshore and offshore. However, disputed oil field ownership and a lack of expert workers still prevent Cambodia from tapping into this resource.

Mining for precious gems is another of Cambodia's key industries, mainly in Ratanakiri for zircon and Pailin for rubies and sapphires. Production has dropped significantly since the early 1990s, however, when the Khmer Rouge was earning around $2 million to $5 million a month from mining activities.

LOGGING

Cambodia's forests are one of the country's most valuable resources. Between 1990 and 2015, some 10.5 million acres (4.25 million ha) of forests—nearly a third of the country's land area—were cut down. Several provinces have been denuded, and the people suffer from shortages of firewood. Increasing domestic and international concerns about excessive logging eventually led to a ban on the export of unprocessed timber in May 1995. Despite this, logging camps in remote areas continued to operate, trucking their timber across the border to Thailand. In November 1995, the International Monetary Fund canceled a loan to Cambodia because of its inadequate forest protection. International pressure has continued to mount, and with large swathes of its forests wiped out, it is more critical than ever for Cambodia to take steps to repair the damage already done.

Timber in Koh Kong province southwest of Phnom Penh

Forest cover increased slightly between 1997 and 2002, but in recent years deforestation has accelerated. The government has taken several steps to protect some forested areas, but illegal logging often continues.

TOURISM

In the 1960s, well over sixty thousand people visited Cambodia every year. At the time, that was an enviable figure for a Southeast Asian country. The outbreak of civil war reduced this source of income to a trickle.

Between 1988 and 1991, for example, only three thousand tourists visited Cambodia each year. Since the signing of the Paris Peace Agreement in 1991, tourists have begun returning in larger numbers, attracted by the historical sites at Angkor Wat. Tourism is now Cambodia's fastest-growing industry.

STRIP MINING

Until recently, trucks used to operate twenty-four hours a day removing earth from Cambodian land and transporting it across the border to Thailand. The earth was deposited in Thailand and then panned for valuable gemstones. The United Nations described the result as a "lunar landscape."

Trade in gemstones was largely in the hands of illegal groups; little of the profits made their way into the mainstream economy of the country. Khmer Rouge units, if not engaging directly in the smuggling of gems out of the country, benefited from the levies they imposed on the trade.

Today, while such illegal activity has more or less ceased, strip mining in the western region along the border with Thailand has had an impact on natural habitats and biodiversity. Residue soil is also washed into the Tonle Sap River, where it adds to the siltation problem.

In 2015, Cambodia welcomed 4.7 million visitors, a 90 percent increase from 2010. Vietnam, its neighbor, had an increase of only 47 percent, even though its total annual visitation is nearly double that of Cambodia. Emerging from the shadow of the Khmer Rouge, much of the country today is open to tourism, although land mines remain buried in more remote areas.

INFRASTRUCTURE

In 2010, Cambodia had an estimated 27,800 miles (44,700 km) of roads, of which only about 2,240 miles (3,600 km) were paved. Many stretches of road were in a state of disrepair. Nevertheless, the situation is improving as rehabilitation projects move forward.

Public transportation is generally limited, although public buses recently started running in Phnom Penh in 2014. There are rail links from Phnom Penh to Battambang and Sihanoukville, but no passenger trains currently run between the cities. There are hopes that the line between Sihanoukville and Phnom Penh will reopen soon.

Inland water transportation is vital in Cambodia; some 1,090 miles (1,750 km) of inland waterways are navigable. The Mekong accounts for

30 percent of this distance, and the Tonle Sap River another 15 percent. The port at Phnom Penh that once could only receive small oceangoing vessels via ports in Vietnam has been upgraded to a deepwater port and now operates independently. Air transportation has expanded, but establishing a national carrier has not been easy. Several different airlines have come and gone due to a lack of commitment, finances, and poor management. Cambodia Angkor Air (established in 2009) and Cambodia Bayon Airlines (established in 2014) are currently the most important airlines, although several others exist with fleet sizes of just a handful of planes.

INDUSTRY

Cambodia has only light industrial factories. These produce household goods, textiles, soft drinks, alcohol, nails, jute sacks, tires, farm tools, pharmaceutical products, cigarettes, and other light consumer goods. The garment industry in particular is important to the economy of Cambodia. It accounts for more than 70 percent of the country's exports, and it employs more than six hundred thousand Cambodians. While low wages remain a concern for international groups and local unions, wages have increased significantly over the past two years.

Most plants operate at low capacity because of periodic shortages of electricity, raw materials, and spare parts. Poor management is also a contributing factor to the low productivity.

Industry accounted for 28 percent of the country's gross domestic product (GDP) in 2015.

CONNECTION TO THE GLOBAL MARKET

Cambodia's principal exports include clothing, footwear, timber, rubber, rice, tobacco, and fishery products. In 2015, the country's total exports amounted to $7.9 billion. Imports, which included motor vehicles, cigarettes, and petroleum products, totaled $10.6 billion. Since 1998, the United States has been Cambodia's largest trade partner, with 23 percent of total exports going to the United States in 2015.

In the last few decades, Cambodia has transitioned into a free market economy and has sought to spur foreign investment. Most foreign investment comes from the countries of Malaysia, China, Taiwan, Vietnam, and South Korea. But the majority of companies are owned exclusively by Cambodians.

Rubber plantations cultivate one of Cambodia's biggest exports.

INTERNET LINKS

www.adb.org/countries/cambodia/economy
The Asian Development Bank offers a short synopsis of the Cambodian economy with a link to a more comprehensive fact sheet.

www.heritage.org/index/country/cambodia
The Heritage Foundation scores countries on their level of economic freedom. It ranks Cambodia compared to other countries around the world and gives some background information on the economy.

www.worldbank.org/en/country/cambodia/overview
The World Bank provides a frequently updated report on the economy of Cambodia as a whole in addition to up-to-date economic data.

ENVIRONMENT

Water is crucial to the Cambodian way of life.

5

THE DIVERSE GEOGRAPHY AND wildlife of Cambodia is a great asset to the country. The abundant supply of fish and water for farming rice is also an integral part of the country's economy. Sadly, the environment is under intense pressure from increased development and deforestation—primarily from illegal logging.

Environmental concerns have often taken a backseat to development in Cambodia. High levels of poverty have attracted the attention of the government more than protecting the environment. Yet this has changed in recent years as the government has tried to slow deforestation. A number of protected areas have been established around the country to protect forests. Logging was banned in 1995; however, illegal logging continues both inside and outside of protected areas. Large land concessions to agricultural plantations since 2000 have also increased the rate of deforestation. The commitment of the government to combat deforestation is often questioned by environmental groups given the lucrative nature of illegal logging.

RAIN FORESTS UNDER THREAT

The major threat to native wildlife in Cambodia is widespread deforestation—an environmental problem that has been escalating over the past couple of decades. Seventy-three percent of Cambodia was covered by forest in 1965. By 2010, just 57 percent of the country was forested, and by 2014 forest cover was down to just 49.5 percent. Vast areas that were once densely covered are now little more than scrublands. Despite bans and restrictions, the government seems to have had little impact on illegal logging.

There are several forces behind continued logging. There is a huge demand for timber to build new houses to replace those that were destroyed during the periods of civil war. The supply of timber has also had to keep pace with an increasing population growth rate, which has raised domestic demand for firewood as well as for housing. Indiscriminate clearing of land for agriculture was common practice during the Pol Pot regime and continues to some extent today. Some forest has also been destroyed through the practice of clearing farmland by burning.

Logging by industrial and small-scale operators has meant the loss of wildlife habitats and a decline in biodiversity. Deforestation in the upper reaches of the Tonle Sap River and around the Tonle Sap Lake is also a likely contributor to siltation, which interferes with spawning, greatly decreasing the number of fish.

A beach at Ream National Park, which was designated as a wildlife refuge in 1993

SAFEGUARDING THE FORESTS

Even though widespread destruction of forests has taken place throughout Cambodia, several parts of the country have been designated protected areas. Cambodia was the first country in Southeast Asia to establish protected areas. In 1925, the forests surrounding the temples of Angkor were declared a national park. By 1969, six wildlife sanctuaries had been established. In 1993, a national system of twenty-three protected areas was set up by royal decree. These areas, which include national parks, wildlife sanctuaries, and protected landscapes, are managed by the Ministry of Environment (MOE) and the Ministry of Agriculture, Forestry, and Fisheries (MAFF).

At the end of 2005, the World Wildlife Fund, together with the MOE and MAFF of Cambodia, announced another two protected areas in the eastern plains of Mondulkiri Province, which is home to many endangered species. In 2016, the Cambodian government created five new protected forests with a total area of 2.5 million acres (1 million ha). The national system of protected areas now covers around 30 percent of the country's total land area.

Many environmental activists believe damming the Mekong River could have devastating consequences.

In recent years, there has been a growing understanding of the contribution of protected areas to the country's development. Making local communities actively involved in and responsible for managing these areas is seen as an effective way to conserve biodiversity, improve fish yields, create sustainable harvests of forest products, and reap the economic potential of ecotourism.

THE HIGH COST OF DAMS

The vital ecosystem supported by the Mekong River is under threat from the construction of hydroelectric dams. Dams built upstream in China, Laos, and Thailand cause problems downstream in Cambodia. The full extent of the environmental impact of these dams is not yet known with certainty, but many environmental experts warn of changes in the natural balance of the river that may throw local wildlife and human communities into chaos.

It was thought that the effect of the dams could influence the river's flow and reduce the annual flooding, which is crucial for fisheries and mangrove swamps. Locals who have depended on the Mekong River for their livelihood

CLIMATE CHANGE: A RISING THREAT

In the near future, climate change—driven by human-produced greenhouse gases—will negatively affect Cambodia in a number of ways. Although climate change is primarily caused by industrialization in high-income countries like the United States and the countries of Europe, it is low-income countries that will pay the highest price.

As temperatures rise, droughts and floods are expected to become more common in Southeast Asia. Unlike some countries, Cambodia does not have the resources available to prepare for these natural disasters. Cambodian farmers will have to deal with the fallout, though they are often already near the poverty line. Floods or droughts can spell disaster for crops and,

Drought has a severe impact on Cambodian villages.

in turn, the finances of families and entire communities who depend on agriculture for a living. Climate change will also make fresh water scarcer around the world. Already, the water level of the Tonle Sap is falling. As this continues, fishermen who ply the lake and farmers who depend on its waters for irrigation will have to change their way of life.

Cambodia is proactively meeting the threat of climate change: it formed a Climate Change Office in 2003 that in 2009 was made into its own department, the Department of Climate Change. Additionally, international donors are providing Cambodia with some funds to prevent the ill effects of climate change. But it remains to be seen whether this will be enough.

for generations have reported changes in the river that they have never witnessed before. The river flows erratically, fluctuating from higher to lower than normal levels. There are fewer fish, and the water—once clear and safe for drinking and bathing—is now murky in some areas.

URBANIZATION AND AIR QUALITY

Air pollution is a growing menace in the face of urbanization. Most Cambodians still live in rural areas, and most households burn firewood for cooking, as it is the most affordable and accessible fuel. Unfortunately, burning firewood releases carbon dioxide into the atmosphere.

Pollution from fuel consumption is also rising as road traffic increases. This is particularly problematic in the capital, Phnom Penh, where traffic jams are becoming common. In addition, most cars and motorcycles are imported secondhand. Being older models, they tend to produce more pollutants, such as sulphur dioxide and benzene.

Industry is another source of air pollution. While Cambodia is not a heavily industrialized country, most of its factories still use old technology—a situation that is unlikely to change without expensive improvements. Since Cambodia's electrical supply is inadequate, many businesses rely on gas-fueled generators for power. Some generators are placed out in the open, and these release harmful gases directly into the atmosphere.

HOSPITAL, FACTORY, AND HOUSEHOLD WASTE

Waste presents a mounting problem in Cambodia. Burning waste releases toxins into the air, while dumping releases toxins into the soil and water.

Medical waste is the biggest hazard to Cambodians and their environment. Cambodia has few incinerators, and many hospitals dispose of their waste—used needles, surgical tools, and body parts, among others—in the city dump, where children living in poverty scavenge daily.

Industrial waste is often discharged into sewers or rivers. Examples of such waste are dyes from the country's many textile factories and chemicals

Cambodia has seven national parks, the largest of which is Virachey National Park. Declared an ASEAN (Association of Southeast Asian Nations) Heritage Site in 2004, it is also the largest protected area in Cambodia, covering 1,235 square miles (3,200 sq km) in the Stung Treng and Ratanakiri provinces.

The park's conservation value is significant on all levels—national and international. It supports a number of endangered wildlife species, such as the tiger, leopard, clouded leopard, Asian elephant, sun bear, gaur, and gibbon. Some of the park's wildlife is found in very few other places.

Water from the park flows into the Mekong River, accounting for about 20 percent of the river's flow. Local residents who live around the park depend on it as a source of fish for food and water for rice **An Asian elephant and her calf** *cultivation. The park is also a rich resource for the locals, who can find their traditional foods and medicines in the mountain forests, as well as plants and animals used in their cultural ceremonies.*

from the photograph developers that are sprouting up all over the capital. While there is a lack of affordable technology, the Ministry of Environment is trying to enforce the installation of treatment plants at larger factories.

Management of household waste has been given a helping hand by international agencies such as the Norwegian Agency for Development Cooperation (NORAD), which has supported the implementation of garbage collection and disposal systems in the capital.

SEWAGE AND CONTAMINATION

Most of Phnom Penh's sewers lead to a long, open drain that empties into a large settlement pond. Sewage from this pond is pumped via the city's ditches into a wetland area, where it eventually feeds into the rivers. Both the settlement pond and the wetland area lie in places where intensive market farming occurs, presenting a high risk of contamination. In some places, the open sewer runs very close to residential areas, and during heavy rains sewage spills into people's backyards.

A lack of funds remains an obstacle to improving sewage management in Phnom Penh. Other towns fare worse, with no central sewage system at all. A treatment plant built in Battambang with money from donors did not function for very long without funds for maintenance. As a result, standards of sanitation remain poor. According to a recent report by the World Health Organization, 60 percent of the rural population and 20 percent of city dwellers do not have a reliable source of potable water.

INTERNET LINKS

www.camclimate.org.kh/en
Cambodia's Department of Climate Change publishes news stories and information about specific policies.

cambodia.panda.org
The Cambodian branch of the World Wildlife Fund presents information about conservation efforts.

www.kh.undp.org/content/cambodia/en/home/operations/projects/ environment_and_energy.html
The United Nations Development Programme outlines the environmental projects it supports in Cambodia.

CAMBODIANS

Cambodia's population is young compared to the median age in Western countries.

MOST CAMBODIANS BELONG TO the Khmer ethnic group. Khmers trace their ancestry back to the builders of Angkor Wat and the Khmer Empire. Minority groups also inhabit Cambodia. Groups of Vietnamese, Chinese, Chams, and indigenous peoples call the country home and have their own cultures that are quite different from the Khmer majority.

As of July 2015, some 15.7 million people lived in Cambodia. Phnom Penh is home to 1.7 million of them, but 79 percent of the population still lives in rural areas. Compare this to the global average of 46 percent. However, urbanization is ongoing in Cambodia. More and more people are leaving the traditional occupations of fishing and farming to live in cities: according to the World Bank, the population of Siem Reap, a city near Angkor Wat, tripled in just ten years between 2000 and 2010.

The population of Cambodia is also quite young. Half of the population is under the age of 24, making this the median age of the country. While this number is low, in 2000 the median age was 17.4, meaning the population is aging quite quickly. Cambodians will need to confront these two issues of rapid urbanization and an aging population in the coming years.

6

"If I want ten, I'll shoot ten (animals), and if I want twenty, I'll shoot twenty."
—Traditional boast of an indigenous hunter

KHMERS

Some 90 percent of Cambodians classify themselves as Khmer. Although their origins are unknown, Khmers likely represent a mixture of Mongol and Melanesian elements. Other accounts suggest that they first came from what is now Malaysia and Indonesia.

On the whole, Khmers are taller and slightly darker skinned than their neighbors, the Thais and the Vietnamese. Khmers have curly hair—it is usually cut short—which also differentiates them from their neighbors. Khmers have intermarried with the other ethnic groups within the country, so there is some variation in physical characteristics.

Until recently, the vast majority of Khmers were content to live in the countryside. The running of small businesses was left to the Chinese and Vietnamese. The Khmer people preferred to work their own farms, where they owned the land themselves and were more or less self-sufficient. Most Khmers still work as farmers, but since 1991, increasing numbers have migrated to Phnom Penh and other urban areas. Moreover, because many Chinese and Vietnamese left Cambodia during the rule of the Khmer Rouge, due to antiforeign bias, Khmers have moved into commercial activities that were once considered alien to them.

Traditionally, Khmers of both sexes wear a loose-fitting wraparound garment called a *sampot* (SAM-pot). Made of cotton or silk, it is a cross between trousers and a dress. A loose jacket or blouse that comes down to about the waist is worn over the sampot. A straw hat, usually pointed, is often worn. A large scarf, known as a *kramar* (cray-MAR), is worn around the neck or the head to protect the skin from the heat and sun.

For everyday work, the traditional form of dress is the sarong (sah-RONG), a length of cloth that is wrapped around the waist. It is worn by both men and women. Shorts are also common among men who work in the countryside. Footwear often consists of loose rubber sandals, but it is not unusual to see men and women walking barefoot.

This Khmer man wears a traditional sarong as he fishes.

VIETNAMESE

The number of Vietnamese living in Cambodia has fluctuated over the years. Under French colonial rule, the Vietnamese were encouraged to settle in the country. Many came, attracted by the opportunities. Before 1970, there were at least 250,000 ethnic Vietnamese living in Cambodia. Under Pol Pot they were forced to flee or, in many cases, were forcibly expelled. They had little choice but to settle in Vietnam—a country that most of them knew little about. After Vietnam invaded Cambodia in late 1978, they began to return. However, many fled after the Vietnamese-backed government lost in Cambodia's May 1993 elections. Today there are an estimated 750,000 Vietnamese in Cambodia.

Some ethnic rivalry exists between the Vietnamese and the Khmers. In part, this springs from the different lifestyles and aspirations of the two groups; the Vietnamese follow a cultural, social, and political order patterned after the Chinese and Confucian systems of organization, while the Khmers follow a loosely structured form of kinship and political organization. The Vietnamese are more work-oriented, partly because Vietnam is a far more

A Hmong farmer and her rice crop

densely populated country. This has forced the Vietnamese to struggle for farmland and to work hard to make a living.

By comparison, Cambodia historically has been a less densely populated country and one where the inhabitants have been able to earn a living more easily.

CHINESE

Chinese immigrants first arrived in Cambodia in the third century BCE. The largest influx occurred in the second half of the nineteenth century and during the twentieth century, mostly from southeastern China. By 1968, there were approximately 250,000 Chinese in Cambodia.

Their economic importance to the country was far greater than their numerical presence might suggest. In many respects, especially in the capital and other towns, they controlled the economic life of the country. Under Pol Pot, however, they were singled out as ideological enemies and persecuted.

Traditionally, the Chinese have made their living as merchants and traders. This made them particularly vulnerable during the Pol Pot years, when any form of business was outlawed.

When the Vietnamese invaded Cambodia in 1978, many Chinese who had managed to survive chose to emigrate. The Vietnamese-backed government severely restricted the rights of the Chinese community—forbidding them from returning to their historical business ventures. A steady exodus of Chinese followed for the next twelve years. In 1990, restrictions on the Chinese were lifted. For the first time they were allowed to celebrate the Chinese New Year and soon Chinese schools opened and Chinese newspapers were published. Since 1993, the number of Chinese people in Cambodia has been growing. Foreign investment by Chinese companies is partly responsible for this change. In 2013, there were an estimated six hundred thousand Chinese in Cambodia.

CHAMS

The Chams are the descendants of a great Champa civilization that was one of the earliest Hindu-influenced states of Southeast Asia. For over one thousand

years, the kingdom of Champa flourished, despite wars with the Chinese and Khmers, until the Vietnamese conquered it in the fifteenth century.

Many of the dispossessed Chams settled in Cambodia, where they managed to avoid servitude under the Vietnamese. In the seventeenth century, the Chams converted to Islam. Under Pol Pot, they were persecuted for not sharing the ideology of the Khmer Rouge.

The dress of the Chams is similar to the Malay dress—a long-sleeved shirt or blouse with pants or an ankle-length skirt, worn in Malaysia and Indonesia. Like the Khmers, men wear sarongs, while women are often seen in long-sleeved jackets.

Current estimates put the number of Chams in Cambodia between half a million and a million. Most live in a couple of hundred villages clustered along the Mekong River to the east and north of the capital. By tradition, Cham men are cattle dealers, fishermen, and boat builders. Cham women are renowned as silk and mat weavers.

The ancient Champa civilization is responsible for the My Son Sanctuary, located in present-day Vietnam.

One group of Khmer Loeu are the Kuy in northern Cambodia. Like many indigenous groups around the world, their population is separated by modern borders. Some live in central Cambodia, while others live in remote areas of Thailand and Laos. Altogether, there are more than half a million Kuy in Southeast Asia.

The Kuy primarily depend on growing rice for food. But they also gather plants and roots from the forest as well as hunt there. They speak the Kuy language and have their own culture, which is very different from the Khmer majority. Additionally, many have animist beliefs: spirits are believed to dwell in nearby mountains, forests, and trees. This has blended with Buddhism in some communities to form a rich spiritual belief system.

Kuy people gather to protest against deforestation of the Prey Lang Forest.

In Cambodia, many live in and around the Prey Lang forest. Prey Lang means "Our Forest" in the Kuy language. Yet the forest is under threat by illegal logging and the sale of some portions for agricultural development. Like many indigenous groups, development and the destruction of the environment threaten their traditional way of life and their livelihoods. In 2016, a large portion of Prey Lang was declared a protected area, but conservationists were disappointed by the omission of some parts of the forest.

KHMER LOEU

A variety of ethnic groups are designated under the term "Khmer Loeu" (meaning "Highland Khmer") because they share the same physical environment—the highland plateaus and valleys, which are heavily forested and surrounded by mountains. Despite their name, they are not closely related to the Khmer. These groups include the Saoch in the Elephant Mountains; the Pear in the Cardamom Mountains; and, along the border with Laos in the northeast, the Krung, Jarai, and Tampuan. The northwest of the country is inhabited by the Kuy.

The various indigenous groups have never integrated with mainstream Cambodian life; this has helped them to preserve their own culture and lifestyle. Because of their geographical isolation, they managed to avoid becoming victims of Pol Pot's genocidal campaigns against ethnic minorities.

The indigenous people have a distinctive appearance because of the importance attached to personal decoration. Their ears are pierced, and the lobes are often elongated to support heavy rings. Heavier bangles are worn around the ankles and wrists. Tattoos are not as common as they once were but are still found.

INTERNET LINKS

cambodianscholars.org/the-cham-people/#
The Cambodian Village Scholars Fund website presents detailed information about the Chams.

minorityrights.org/minorities/khmer-leou
Minority Rights Group International gives details about the history of the Khmer Loeu, as well as contemporary problems they face.

www.tourismcambodia.com/about-cambodia/khmer-people.htm
This government-sponsored site breaks down the ethnic composition of Cambodia and describes the various ethnic groups.

LIFESTYLE

Farming shapes the lifestyle of most Cambodians.

7

LIFE IN CAMBODIA REMAINS QUITE traditional. Most of the population still lives outside of the urban centers. The primary occupation is rice farming, which means people align their lives to the cycles of planting and harvesting. Although the Cambodian government has tried to improve health care and education in recent years, they still do not measure up to the standards of many Western countries.

Many Cambodians do not live close to hospitals or secondary schools. In 2013, just 22.5 percent of Cambodian households had access to electricity, making life there very different from life in the West. Despite these differences, there are many similarities between the culture of Cambodia and Western cultures. Family plays an integral role in the lives of Cambodians, and important ceremonies like weddings and funerals mark important occasions in family life.

THE TRADITIONAL WORLDVIEW

Meditation is a key part of Buddhists' lives.

There is a traditional Cambodian attitude toward life that is the result of centuries of Buddhist teaching. The present life is viewed as only one stage in a broader cycle of life where one is repeatedly reborn. Consequently, there is a tendency to accept one's present situation in life as somewhat preordained. The idea that one ought to work hard in order to make more money and improve the quality of life is at odds with traditional Cambodian beliefs. Working to provide sufficient food for oneself and one's family is seen in Buddhist terms as an end in itself. Being ambitious is not necessarily regarded as virtuous.

Similarly, there is a belief system that discourages feelings of envy toward those who have more money or possessions. It has been observed that such a philosophy allows the poor to remain poor, while allowing a more privileged minority to escape responsibility for society at large. Part of the extreme ideology of the Khmer Rouge was a total rejection of this philosophical acceptance of inequality. Pol Pot stood for egalitarianism in a very literal way; his ideas were a radical rejection of a traditional lifestyle that had governed the country for centuries.

The traditional Buddhist attitude to life was not destroyed by Pol Pot's regime. It is still evident today and helps to explain the great importance that is still attached to personal relationships. Showing respect for one's family relations, especially those who are older, is still an integral part of a young person's upbringing. In theory at least, it is extended to society at large.

LIFE AFTER THE KILLING FIELDS

War has had a profound impact on the Cambodian experience. So many men died during the years of war that women have taken over new areas of employment. Before the 1970s, a number of occupations—shopkeepers, village administrators, and government officials—were male bastions. War and revolution have transformed these patterns of employment, and today women have taken on a variety of new roles.

Men have also found their traditional patterns of employment affected by the years of turmoil and killing. Many jobs of a commercial nature—especially small businesses and shops—were traditionally reserved for the Chinese and Vietnamese. These people suffered under Khmer Rouge rule, and many who were fortunate enough to survive were anxious to leave the country after the Vietnamese pulled out in the early 1990s. Cambodian men, accustomed to thinking these jobs were beyond their abilities, are now succeeding as small businessmen and shopkeepers and in growth industries such as tourism.

This memorial commemorates the lives of those who died in the killing fields.

A deadly vacuum was created by the virtual extermination of the country's middle-class professionals by the Khmer Rouge. When some semblance of order was restored by the Vietnamese invasion, there was a need to repopulate—literally—the capital of Phnom Penh. Many Khmers of rural descent, with little or no previous experience of city life, found themselves drawn into an urban lifestyle for the first time.

The United Nations organized the resettlement of over 360,000 people from six refugee camps in Thailand. About 5 percent of the population had

Although most Cambodians do not have access to electricity at home, 94 percent of Cambodians own at least one cell phone as of 2015 (13 percent own more than one phone!). Around 39.5 percent of Cambodians own a smartphone (Samsung is the most popular brand, followed by Apple). The rise of smartphones in recent years has also resulted in many more Cambodians being able to access the internet: in 2012, just 5 percent of Cambodians could access the internet, but in 2015 more than 30 percent reported having access to the internet. This change is largely due to smartphones, which allow people without the means to own a personal computer access to the internet. As you might expect, the primary reason that Cambodians go online is for entertainment. Watching movies, listening to music, and going on social media sites are popular activities among Cambodians and people in the Western world alike. In fact, most Cambodians report that they have only accessed social media like Facebook on a smartphone, never on a personal computer. Despite the fact that most Cambodians primarily use the internet for entertainment, internet access also has the potential to transform life in Cambodia. Farmers in rural Cambodia can now connect to people around the world. This opens up economic opportunities for Cambodians, as well as creates a chance for people from diverse cultures to connect with one another.

Most villages have a *sala* (SAR-la), or open pavilion, which is used for general meetings or as a temporary shelter for visitors.

fled to these camps over the years, and they were shifted back to Cambodia in 1992 and 1993. The original terms offered to the refugees were very generous: they were allowed to choose their location and received sufficient land to grow rice, the materials for building a house, and the necessary farming and domestic tools to begin a new life.

Unfortunately, too many of the refugees chose to resettle in the Battambang region because this was the most prosperous agricultural part of the country. There was not sufficient land to go around so the United Nations was forced to offer other terms. Many refugees were persuaded to settle in other parts of the countryside or to move to towns where small businesses could be started. Instead of land, returnees were offered a cash payment of $50.

RURAL HOUSES

The typical home in the countryside is built by the family who lives in it. The general shape is rectangular and the floor is supported above the ground by wooden stilts. The space between the ground and the wooden floor is between 5 and 10 feet (1.5 and 3 m), the actual size depending on the degree of flooding that is anticipated, as well as the prosperity of the home builders. Larger and stronger wooden piles are more expensive.

A traditional house in Kampong Thom

The roof is inexpensively thatched, using locally available leaves from palm trees or dried savannah grass. Large protruding eaves are constructed as a means of keeping the walls dry during the monsoon rains. The walls themselves are put together by overlapping panels of timber or woven bamboo that are attached to the posts holding up the roof. At least one of the walls will have an open window space that is covered by a thick mat during heavy rainfall.

A typical indigenous village has a character that is a little different from the usual Cambodian rural settlement. The village is laid out in a circular shape, with an outer ring of huts for married couples. A smaller ring of huts inside this circumference is for unmarried villagers and village guests. In the center of the village, there is usually a communal long house where the elders gather for discussion and decision making.

LIFE ON THE FARM

A farm family rises at dawn, summoned by the crowing of the cocks from beneath the house, where they share the living space with other fowl, a pig or two, and the household oxen.

After the family washes in a barrel of rainwater with the aid of a coconut shell ladle, breakfast is prepared and consumed. The husband then departs

The annual farming cycle is broadly determined by the process of growing rice. The grains of rice that will be used for planting are dried in the sun, then planted in nurseries. It is then necessary to prepare small ditches to carry the water that is so essential to the growth of the plant.

After the seeds sprout, they are transplanted by gathering bundles of the stems and soaking them for two or three days in a corner of the field. Oxen are used to plow and prepare the fields. Each seedling is then planted in the plowed mud. Between the months of May and October, there is a

Planting rice (*above*) is a labor-intensive process; harvesting rice also requires significant time and effort.

constant need to remove weeds, which would otherwise choke the growing rice.

The end of the rainy season—around October—is the time to harvest the rice. Farmers work together to help cut, tie, and thresh the crop. The threshing is done by hand, and the separated grain is carefully collected. The wasted stalks are gathered and later used as fertilizer for the soil. Each farm household keeps sufficient rice to feed itself for a year. The remainder is sold for cash to a government-run office.

Between early 1979 and 1989, rice farming was managed collectively by "solidarity groups." Each production team consisted of about fifteen households and was responsible for working 24 to 36 acres (10–15 ha) of land. After the Vietnamese withdrawal, rice farming reverted back to private and family-based production.

with his packed lunch for a day's work in the fields owned by his family. The children have their breakfast and prepare for a day at school, one that is likely to be run by Buddhist monks and that may be located near the local temple. Most children walk to school.

During the day, the woman of the house prepares food, feeds the farm animals, and washes the family clothes. At night the home is lit by an oil lamp. The family spends the evening together and retires early, before 10 p.m. Festivals and religious events at the local temple are the main interruptions to this pattern of life.

THE INDIGENOUS PEOPLE'S WAY OF LIFE

In the remote Ratanakiri Province, over 200 miles (322 km) from the capital, 66 percent of the population belong to indigenous ethnic groups (as of 2013). They consist of eight different ethnic groups, and their lifestyle has continued unchanged for centuries. Slash-and-burn agriculture supports the farming of rice and the growing of a few vegetables. Water buffalo and cows are raised in small numbers.

Selling of surplus rice is the main way of raising cash. Dangerous work such as mining for semiprecious stones that are then sold to visiting Chinese or Khmer traders presents such a possibility as well. Such work is risky because the caves are usually unexplored. It is not uncommon for miners to lose their way and become trapped or to die from sudden rockfalls caused by primitive mining methods.

Most villagers in the remote northeast have no interest in politics. Names like Pol Pot and Norodom Sihanouk mean nothing to the typical indigenous villager. Yet ironically, the province of Ratanakiri was one of the most heavily bombed provinces during the Vietnam War.

The Ho Chi Minh Trail passed through the region and was consequently carpet bombed by Americans. In the early 1970s, Pol Pot located his main base in the province. For the indigenous people, though, national politics wins little attention. Working in the fields with a cane rucksack that carries the day's lunch is the norm.

Folk medicine is still practiced in Cambodia, especially among the indigenous people. A common practice is to lubricate the skin covering the affected part of the body and rub it briskly with a copper token. The rubbing is done in a direction away from the head of the sick person. The theory is that the "bad" blood comes to the surface. The tokens used are usually family heirlooms.

LIFE IN PHNOM PENH

The capital city, Phnom Penh, is the only place in Cambodia where an urban lifestyle has firmly taken root. *Phnom* comes from the Khmer word for "hill," while *Penh* was the name of a devout woman who, in the eighteenth century, had a small temple constructed on the summit.

The influence of the French is still evident in the broad tree-shaded avenues and old colonial buildings around the city. Recent investments by foreign companies have added some modernity to the town—advertisements with familiar consumer brand names now deck public places—and people, especially men, tend to dress in Western clothes. Compared with other capital cities, even those in other parts of Asia, the pace of life is never fast. The lifestyle of most Cambodian urban dwellers remains a very calm and relaxed one.

HEALTH AND WELL-BEING

In 1977, at the height of the Khmer Rouge's power, the average life expectancy in Cambodia was just 19.5 years. War and genocide had taken a terrible toll on the population. But as of 2015, average life expectancy is up to 68.7 years—just ten and a half years shy of the average life expectancy of people in the United States. Since 1993, Cambodia has made impressive gains in improving public health: child mortality has declined; access to health care has improved; and major diseases like tuberculosis, malaria, and HIV/AIDS are less likely to be fatal. Despite these important steps, more improvements need to be made. Access to health care is still unequal, and indigenous groups in particular often do not have health care facilities available to them.

The following figures, from data gathered in 2015, summarize the difficult situation that still exists in Cambodia today:

- The infant mortality rate is 25 per 1,000 live births (this is more than neighboring Thailand and Vietnam, but less than Laos and Myanmar);
- The maternal mortality rate in childbirth is 1.6 for every 1,000 live births; and
- Only 40 percent of the population in rural areas and 20 percent in Phnom Penh have access to safe drinking water.

Cambodia was once one of the least developed countries with regards to public health, but it now stands near the middle of the pack in Southeast Asia.

EDUCATION

For years, completion of the educational curriculum was one of the few alternatives to peasant life in Cambodia. Success in education meant gaining a diploma. This allowed the holder to obtain an administrative position in a sprawling bureaucracy that was based in the towns but that extended its influence and control into the countryside as well.

As in other areas of Cambodian life, the ideology of the Khmer Rouge showed a radical rejection of traditional academic systems in the life of the country's citizens. Anyone with a diploma was condemned as an "intellectual" and sentenced to hard labor or even executed.

The Khmer Rouge destroyed every textbook along with all school equipment and facilities. Education was condemned as corrupt; schools were replaced with indoctrination programs that sought to spread Pol Pot's ideology. Before 1975, there were about twenty thousand teachers in Cambodia, but by 1979 there were only about five thousand left. The rest had either died or fled the country.

Beginning in the 1990s, there has been a massive effort to make up for lost time. Great strides have been made in improving education. As of 2015, 96 percent of young children are enrolled in primary school, and the adult literacy rate is almost 75 percent. But there are still problems with the educational system. Many rural areas do not have secondary schools, which means most children do not have the opportunity to attend high school.

Additionally, there is a shortage of teachers in the country, which results in a teacher to student ratio of 1:47. For comparison, the ratio is 1:14 in the United States. This shortage of teachers and secondary schools means the education of Cambodia still has a great deal of room for improvement despite the large gains that have been made since the end of the Khmer Rouge.

WOMEN AND FAMILY

A primary school class in Siem Reap

When a Cambodian woman marries, she keeps her maiden name. Women have traditionally been regarded as active partners in a marriage. They bring up the children and run the home. They also take charge of the family's domestic budget and are responsible for the purchase of food.

The important role that women play in a marriage is clearly reflected in the Cambodian proverb "If you are a colonel, your wife is a general." Another telling reminder of the respect accorded to women lies in the fact that the family riches—in the form of precious stones—are in the personal care of women.

The riches may take the form of personal jewelry that is worn by the woman when she is not working in the fields or the house. Traditionally, the family jewels are kept wrapped up and brought out only on special occasions.

The years under Pol Pot and the warfare that engulfed the country before and after this regime were extremely difficult ones for Cambodian women as well as men. As more and more men were killed and maimed, women were left with the sole responsibility for bringing up the children.

When Pol Pot emptied the towns of their entire populations and enforced a collective form of agriculture, women were often separated from their children, further splintering the Cambodian family.

THE WEDDING CEREMONY

The civil marriage ceremony is not really a ceremony at all. It consists of little more than the bride and bridegroom presenting their birth certificates to a local official and declaring their willingness to be registered as married. A traditional wedding, on the other hand, is an occasion for festivities. If the parents of the bride or bridegroom adhere to tradition, the day for the wedding is decided according to the horoscopes of the couple. In addition, the groom must also prepare a dowry for his bride, which represents his gratitude to the bride's parents for bringing her up.

Whether in the countryside or the towns, weddings are a time for dancing and eating. In Phnom Penh, families who can afford to do so erect an awning in front of their house, with tables and chairs set out on the pavement for guests. In the countryside, a temporary shed is often erected. The food is cooked outside in large pots over gas burners. Depending on the families, weddings may take from one day to several days. Traditionally, a scarf is given to "fix the words and tie the hearts" of the newly married couple.

INTERNET LINKS

www.commisceo-global.com/country-guides/cambodia-guide
Commisceo Global gives information about Cambodian culture and etiquette.

www.usaid.gov/cambodia/education
US Aid examines the current state of education in Cambodia.

www.worldbank.org/en/country/cambodia
The World Bank provides links to recent stories about projects to improve health care and education in Cambodia.

RELIGION

Statues of the reclining Buddha represent the spiritual figure right before his death. These statues are a common motif in Buddhist art.

BUDDHISM DOMINATES THE spiritual landscape of Cambodia. Nearly 97 percent of Cambodians are Buddhist, while 2 percent are Muslim and less than 1 percent are Christian. This makes Cambodia the most devoutly Buddhist country in the world—no other country has such a high percentage of Buddhists, despite the fact that the Khmer Rouge tried to stamp out Buddhism during its reign.

Buddhism is very different from other organized religions like Christianity and Islam. The founder of Buddhism, often simply referred to as the Buddha (or "Enlightened One"), never claimed to be more than a normal human being. The Buddha did not profess to be a divine messenger or the recipient of holy texts. Instead, he asserted that suffering could be overcome through living a life of goodness and contemplation. He did not ask for people to have faith that he was telling the truth, but rather invited them to follow the path he had discovered and see for themselves if their lives improved.

Today, there are hundreds of millions of Buddhists in the world, and Southeast Asia is the region of the world with the highest percentage of Buddhists. Buddhism remains a central part of daily life for most Cambodians who spend time at temples and donate food to Buddhist monks.

THE BUDDHA

Prince Gautama Siddhartha was born into a wealthy ruling family in what is now Nepal in the sixth century BCE. Around the age of thirty, he gave up his life of luxury, left his wife and the court behind him, and renounced all earthly ambitions. For six years, he practiced an extremely austere life, fasting until he was weak with hunger.

Eventually he came to realize that the road to enlightenment lay not through a life of denial, but through meditation. Legend records how he experienced enlightenment one day when he was sitting in meditation under a fig tree near Bodh Gaya, a village in India.

For the next four decades he led the life of a teacher, showing through example how to practice the good life that leads to enlightenment.

THE SPREAD OF BUDDHISM

Following the Buddha's death, his teachings gradually spread across India. Beginning in the seventh and eighth centuries, the Buddha's beliefs were persecuted within India. The Indian states that supported Buddhism were eventually conquered by Muslim rulers, and Buddhism ceased to be a major religion in India by the thirteenth century. By then, it had been spread by monks to present-day Sri Lanka, Tibet, and most of Southeast Asia. In all these countries it is still an influential religion with millions of devout followers.

During the early period of Buddhism's growth, a major schism occurred because of different interpretations given to the philosophy. The disagreement has resulted in a permanent division of Buddhism into Mahayana and Theravada.

The form of Buddhism that came to flourish in Cambodia was Theravada, "the Way of the Elders." In the view of many scholars, this is regarded as

This Sri Lankan representation of the Buddha demonstrates the religion's vast reach in ancient times.

closer to the original teachings of the Buddha than the Mahayana tradition. Mahayana Buddhism is found mostly in Tibet, Nepal, Korea, Japan, and parts of China.

BUDDHIST BELIEFS

Buddhism has no belief in an omnipotent god. Neither is there a belief in an afterworld where one spends eternity after death. Both concepts relate to the idea of a beginning (god) and an end (heaven), but Buddhism is best understood in terms of a circle, rather than a straight line with beginning and ending points.

What this means for the individual believer is that one's present life is merely a stage in an ongoing progression. Death is seen as both the end of one stage of life and the beginning of another stage. The individual is reborn in a new form, and not always as a human. Eventually, it is hoped, the individual will reach a final state of enlightenment known as nirvana. Nirvana brings about the end of the cycle of rebirth.

BUDDHISM IN CAMBODIA

For many centuries, Buddhism was inextricably woven into the texture of Cambodian life. It was a vital part of the Cambodians' sense of cultural and national identity. Buddhism found its way into the daily pattern of people's lives and affected their lives on many different levels. It characterized and shaped their attitude to life on a philosophical level while also, more practically, determining the way they celebrated their holidays and provided opportunities for family reunions.

The overwhelming majority of Cambodians are Buddhists. Before the Khmer Rouge took over in 1975, there were over three thousand monasteries in the country and more than sixty-four thousand monks. Life in the countryside was closely bound to the local temple, and monks were highly respected figures.

Pol Pot's regime disbanded all the temples, and Buddhist monks became prime targets of persecution. The vast majority of the monks were executed

The Buddha named his path "the Middle Way." This referred to his rejection of the two extremes of hedonism (the pursuit of pleasure) and rigid asceticism (the pursuit of pain).

THE PATH TO NIRVANA

The ultimate goal of Buddhist practice is the cessation of suffering—nirvana. The Noble Eightfold Path is the means by which people can reach that goal according to Buddhist beliefs. It is made up of eight steps that are to be practiced and perfected simultaneously over many years.

The first two parts of the path fall under the category of wisdom:
- *Right view: holding the central beliefs of Buddhist, that beings are reborn after death, karma affects one's life, and nirvana can be achieved*
- *Right resolve: dedication to Buddhist practice*

The next three concern moral conduct:
- *Right speech: not telling lies, but also not engaging in harmful speech or gossip*
- *Right action: not stealing, harming others, or acting in any other injurious way*
- *Right livelihood: not harming others or cheating for one's employment*

The last three relate to meditation:
- *Right effort: striving to meditate*
- *Right mindfulness: to be present in the moment when meditating*
- *Right concentration: concentrating effectively—this is only possible through repeated meditation practice*

The path culminates in nirvana. Buddhists believe it may take more than one lifetime of practice to reach this goal. Monks are forbidden from discussing their own level of spiritual achievement toward enlightenment with lay people, but it is clear that only the most senior practitioners would claim enlightenment.

or died from overwork and lack of food while being forced to work in the countryside. Perhaps as few as two thousand monks survived the Pol Pot years of 1975 to 1979.

According to Khmer Rouge ideology, Buddhism was merely a way of deceiving people. Pol Pot's minister for education declared in 1978 that "under the old regime, peasants believed in Buddhism, which the ruling class utilized as a propaganda instrument."

Attempting to wipe out all Buddhist beliefs and practices in one violent stroke was psychologically and culturally traumatic. The same minister for education complacently declared that "with the development of revolutionary consciousness, the people stopped believing and the monks left the temples. The problem is gradually extinguished. Hence there is no problem." For the average Cambodian, however, this was a destabilizing shift.

Despite this horrific persecution, Buddhism was revived in 1979 with the help of Vietnamese monks who came to Cambodia and began to ordain new monks. Buddhism has since found its way back into Cambodian society, with an estimated sixty thousand monks in 2005 and many temples restored or rebuilt.

MONKS' ORDINATION

There are more than fifty thousand Buddhist monks in Cambodia. It is difficult to be sure of the exact number because many Cambodian men become monks for a short amount of time before disrobing. Unlike many other religious traditions, there is no expectation that a monk will remain a

These young monks wear the traditional saffron robe.

monk for life. In fact, most men hope to be a monk for at least a small part of their lives. Only a few Cambodians decide to become monks for their whole life. Most enter a temple for a few months or less, before returning to their normal working life.

A common practice is for a young man to take temporary Buddhist vows at some stage between leaving school and getting married. There is an ordination ceremony that is held before the beginning of Vassa, the monastic period of prayer that coincides with the rainy season. During his time as a novice monk, a young man leads a simple life based upon the Buddha's renunciation of wealth and luxury. As a result, the young man improves his karma and increases his spiritual worthiness. The immediate family of the young man also accrues spiritual merit and feels suitably proud when a close relative dons the saffron (orange) robe.

In order to become a monk for life, a man must be a bachelor and older than twenty-one years of age. It is assumed that he will have studied Buddhism for a number of years. The decision to enter a temple on a permanent basis is purely a personal choice. At any stage, a monk can reconsider his decision and return to secular life.

Monks are a common sight in Cambodia. Unlike Christian monks, their lives take them outside their monasteries on a daily basis. Buddhist monks go on a daily alms round to receive their one meal of the day from nearby lay people. This ensures they are part of the nearby community and gives Buddhist lay people the opportunity to make merit by donating food. Monks are also forbidden from preparing food so that they can focus on a life of spiritual contemplation.

THE MONASTIC LIFE

A temple complex is composed of a small number of buildings enclosed by a wall with a main entrance. The main building is the temple itself, which contains the chief Buddha statue. There are also living quarters for the resident monks and a few open hall areas.

The daily routine for a Buddhist monk begins with an early morning period of meditation and prayer. This is followed by a walking journey

Tep Vong

Theravada Buddhism is the dominant religion in Cambodia. Yet it is not a uniform religion that is united under one leader like Catholicism is under the pope. Rather, there are many different sects with their own leaders and hierarchy. In Cambodia, there are two major sects: the Maha Nikaya, the larger of the two, and the Dhammayuttika Nikaya. Cambodian monks belong to one of these two groups. Each group is led by a supreme patriarch. Historically, these have been the highest-ranking Buddhist monks in Cambodia, but in 2006 this changed. For the first time in more than 150 years, a great supreme patriarch, Tep Vong, was appointed as the leader of both sects. Tep Vong was one of the seven senior monks who helped the Vietnamese reestablish Buddhism in Cambodia after the fall of the Khmer Rouge.

This Vietnamese-backed government would later become the current ruling Cambodian's People Party (CPP). Some critics say that Tep Vong's elevation to great supreme patriarch was a political move due to his close ties with the CPP. Tep Vong publically defends the CPP and criticizes opposition parties and leaders for not following the CPP. Just like the rest of the world, in Cambodia politics and religion can often intermingle.

WOMEN AND BUDDHISM

Women cannot become monks in the same way as men, but they are allowed to live in temples as lay nuns. Lay nuns wear white robes, and their heads are usually shaved. There are approximately one thousand lay nuns in Cambodia. While women were able to ordain in the same way as men during the Buddha's own lifetime, and for approximately 1,500 years after his death, the lineage of Theravada nuns was broken when there were no surviving nuns to ordain new ones. This led to the current situation in Cambodia where fully ordained nuns no longer exist. There have been efforts in Sri Lanka and other Buddhist countries to restart the lineage of fully ordained nuns, but these efforts have not taken place in Cambodia to date. As a result, there are often less financial support and educational opportunities for Cambodian nuns when compared to Cambodian monks.

This Buddhist nun is holding prayer bracelets intended for temple goers.

In the eyes of many, women who choose to reside in a temple to study Buddhism and meditate are often purer in their motives than their male counterparts. For young men, joining a temple as a novice monk is sometimes as much a social convention as a religious calling. There is also undoubted social esteem that accompanies the act of entering a monastery for most men. This is not the case for women. Therefore, when a woman chooses to enter a temple, it is often because she is drawn to the teachings of Buddhism.

in the neighborhood for the purpose of collecting food for the day. Monks take a vow to eat only before noon and refrain from food for the remainder of the day. After eating, there is further time for meditation and time for chores such as cleaning the temple. Some monks also study religious texts and elder monks will give Dharma talks—explanations of Buddhist practice and encouragement for Buddhist practitioners. Life in a temple is highly regimented—there are a total of 227 rules that monks must follow, such as not creating disagreements or not eating between noon and sunrise.

BUDDHISM IN PRACTICE

Most Cambodians are Buddhists and are aware of their religion's equivalent of the Christian Ten Commandments. These general rules for good living prohibit the taking of life, stealing, committing adultery, drinking alcohol, and telling falsehoods.

The ordinary Cambodian is not striving to reach nirvana, the ultimate goal of Buddhism that spells the end of the cycle of rebirth. It would be more realistic to say that the ordinary Cambodian Buddhist is content to try to improve the quality of his or her spiritual life by accumulating merit in their present existence. Sufficient merit will improve their chances when it comes to rebirth. In this respect, at least, Buddhism bears some resemblance to the Christian idea that a person's behavior and choices in this life will determine what happens in the next world.

A representation of the Buddha is found in most Cambodian homes and shops, usually in the form of a statue placed on a shelf or in a small alcove. Alongside this formal acknowledgement to Buddhism, there is also a widespread belief in ancestor worship and the existence of local spirits. It is not uncommon to see Cambodians wearing small charms, which are believed to protect them from unhelpful spirits. In the countryside especially, it is often thought that an illness might be due to the malign influence of a spirit. Treating an illness is often a combination of taking medicine and engaging in folk magic to drive out evil spirits.

ISLAM

Phnom Penh's mosque

One of the main minority religions in Cambodia is Islam. The country's Muslims are mostly descended from the Chams, who came from what is now central Vietnam after the decisive defeat of the Champa kingdom by the Vietnamese in 1471.

Islam, together with Buddhism, Hinduism, and Christianity, is one of the four major religions of the world. It has an estimated 1.6 billion believers worldwide. The Middle East, where Islam was founded by the Prophet Muhammad in the seventh century, has traditionally been the stronghold of the religion. Sizable populations are also found in Indonesia, which is the country with the largest number of Muslims living in it, India, Pakistan, Bangladesh, China, Nigeria, and the United States.

The Chams are devout Muslims. Many have performed the hajj (HAHJ), or pilgrimage to the holy city of Mecca, Saudi Arabia, where the Kaaba, or House of Allah, is located. It is the duty of every Muslim to visit Mecca at least once in his or her lifetime, unless prevented from doing so by reason of poverty or illness.

One interesting way in which Cambodian Islam has been influenced by the dominant religion of Buddhism lies in the manner devotees are called to prayer. Generally, across the Islamic world, the faithful are called to prayer by the chanting of the *muezzin* (moo-EZ-in), the person tasked with reciting the call to prayer, from the mosque. In Cambodia, however, the call is announced by the beating of a drum—just as in Buddhist pagodas.

Unfortunately, along with Buddhism in Cambodia, Islam was ruthlessly suppressed between 1975 and 1979, under the Khmer Rouge, and members of the Cham Muslim community were executed as a matter of policy.

CHRISTIANITY

The Roman Catholic Church in Cambodia consists of the Apostolic Vicariate of Phnom Penh and the Apostolic Prefectures of Battambang and Kampong Cham.

Cambodia has an estimated twenty-five thousand Roman Catholics. Like Buddhism and Islam, Christianity was banned in 1975 by the Khmer Rouge. The right of Christians to meet to worship was not restored until 1990.

Protestantism is a growing influence in Cambodia due to evangelical efforts of missionary groups that started in the 1980s and grew in the 1990s. The missionaries often offer material aid, such as food, to the Cambodians. This outreach has been pointed out as a possible reason for conversion to Christianity.

This church floats in the Tonle Sap.

INTERNET LINKS

www.cambodia-travel.com/khmer/religion.htm
This article discusses the history of religion in Cambodia.

asia.isp.msu.edu/wbwoa/southeast_asia/cambodia/religion.htm
The Asian Studies Center at Michigan State University takes an in-depth look at religion in Cambodia.

www.tourismcambodia.com/about-cambodia/religion.htm
The official government website for tourism offers an overview of Theravada Buddhism in Cambodia.

LANGUAGE

The walls of Prasat Kravan temple show the beauty of Khmer writing.

9

LINGUISTICALLY, CAMBODIA IS A remarkably homogenous society. Some 90 percent of Cambodians speak Khmer as a first language. However, there are many other important languages in Cambodia in addition to Khmer. Sizeable minority communities of Vietnamese, Chinese, and indigenous peoples speak and write their own languages. Additionally, French, the colonial language of the country, left an imprint on Cambodian society. It is still spoken by some of the older generations. Recently, English has also increased in prominence due to its use as a language of international commerce.

The linguistic landscape of Cambodia is quite diverse. This is reflected not only in the speech of Cambodians but also in the media and education of the country. In the future, it is likely that the importance of English will increase as Cambodia becomes more integrated into the global market. Khmer will undoubtedly remain the most frequently spoken language and an important symbol of Cambodian unity.

The word for the Cambodian currency—the riel—is derived from a small silver carp that is the staple of the Cambodian diet, a testimony to the importance of fishing in Cambodia.

THE WAR ON THE WRITTEN WORD

Under Pol Pot, the written form of language was systematically destroyed. Schools were closed down, and writing was regarded as redundant in the agricultural society that was being imposed across the whole country. Anyone identified as a journalist by the Khmer Rouge was executed. Books were routinely burned, not because they contained uncomfortable ideas but because they were books. By 1978, there were very few books to be found anywhere in Cambodia. Under Pol Pot, the National Library was converted to a stable. Today, decades later, it contains more than one hundred thousand books, a sign that Cambodians are reading and writing once more.

AUSTROASIATIC LANGUAGES

The Austroasiatic language family is made up of a large number of languages and dialects that are spoken by different cultures across Southeast Asia. The most widely spoken language in this family is Vietnamese, which is spoken by more than 75 million people. The second largest is Khmer, spoken by some 13.6 million Cambodians and more than 2 million people outside of Cambodia.

THE KHMER LANGUAGE

The Khmer language has two styles of writing. One is an angular form, called *chrieng* (KRU-ng); the other is a rounded script, called *mul* (MUL), which is reserved for special decorative occasions. The written form can be traced back many centuries to the Indian influence on the country. Even if one is unable to understand or even pronounce any of the words, the Khmer script is a beautiful example of calligraphy. It is written from left to right with no space between words.

There is only a present tense in the language; a reference to the past or the future is made by adding a suitable word to the sentence. For example, the tense of "I cooked the food" is conveyed by saying "I cook the food yesterday" or "I cook the food already."

Unlike some Asian languages, there are no tones in the Khmer language.

On the other hand, there are twenty-three vowel sounds (there are fifteen in English) and thirty-three consonants. Each vowel has two sounds that depend on the consonant associated with it.

The spoken form of the language today incorporates a number of words of French, Vietnamese, and Chinese origin. Many military and government words, like "police" and "field marshal," have their origin in the French of colonial rule.

The language of the Chinese, who were influential for so long in the commercial life of the country, has retained a strong presence. Some Cambodian words for numbers—"thirty" and "forty," for instance—are derived from Chinese. Many Cambodian words for the terms of weights and measures are also Chinese in origin.

This sign welcoming visitors to Kampot province features English and Khmer script.

LANGUAGE AND CULTURE

The language of a culture is inseparable from the pattern of life that makes up that culture. In one classic example, the Inuit of North America and Greenland have dozens of words for snow and ice because they are such an important part of their lives.

The same is true of the Cambodian language when naming rice. Simple distinctions like "steamed rice" and "boiled rice" appear as very crude in a language that has more than one hundred different words for different types of rice. A culture that is so very dependent on rice has quite naturally developed a language precise enough to account for all its varieties and shades of difference.

The Cambodian language reflects the preciseness with which a culture's language can respond to its circumstances. There is, for instance, a word that means "a small animal tucking in its legs as it runs and turns at a sharp angle," telling of the fact that Cambodia is predominantly an agricultural society.

What follows can only provide a very approximate guide to the pronunciation of Khmer. Westerners find the language an especially difficult one to master, and Western linguists readily admit that it does present challenges. For example, there are eight different letters that correspond to sounds that register somewhere between the t and d sound of English. There are four distinct letters that can only be represented in English by the ch sound.

Numbers

pee (PEE). . . . . two

bram (BRAM) . . . . five

bram-pee (BRAM-PEE) . . . . seven

Greetings

Joom reab suor (JEWM RE-a SUE-o) . . . . . . Hello

Lear heouy (LEA HOY). . . . . Good-bye

Suom tous (SUE-um too). . . . . Excuse me

Basics

Bat (BAH) (used by men) . . . . Yes

Jas (JAHS) (used by women). . . . . Yes

Suom (SUE-um) . . . . Please

Ar kun (R KUN). . . . . Thank you

The Cambodian language also reflects the complex personal relationships in Cambodian society. In English, it is possible to say "How do you do?" or "How are you?" to address any person. In Cambodian, there are a number of different words for "you," and their usage depends on the social relationship that is seen to exist between the speaker and the person being addressed.

There is one class of words to address close family members, and even within this group there are different words for older relations—who are due more respect—and younger brothers or sisters. There are specific terms for addressing a monk, and whenever a member of the royal family is being referred to, there are other special terms of address.

REGIONAL VARIETIES OF SPEECH

The Cambodian language has accent differences according to the background of the speaker. The language as spoken by Khmers is not identical in its pronunciation to that spoken by people in the remote northwest of the country. There are also noticeable differences between rural and urban accents. The word for "mother" is pronounced "may" in the countryside, while urban dwellers are more inclined to pronounce the word as "ma."

An account by a survivor of the Khmer Rouge years relates how she felt constantly endangered by the fact that she had been brought up in Phnom Penh. As a former resident of the capital, she knew that the Khmer Rouge would regard her as probably middle class and therefore an ideological enemy. One of the first steps she took to disguise her background was to change her accent and pronounce words in the manner of a country person.

MINORITY LANGUAGES

The Cham people, who live in parts of both Cambodia and Vietnam, have their own language. It can still be found written in the traditional Cham alphabet (derived from a script from India), although this is becoming increasingly rare. A Romanized script introduced by the French is far more common today.

In Cambodia, most Chams have remained Muslims, unlike the Chams of Vietnam, who have adopted the religion and language of the Vietnamese. The Cambodian Chams' adherence to their religion helps preserve not only their separate cultural traditions but also their language. Although nearly all Chams speak fluent Cambodian, they have preserved their own language by using it at home.

Various indigenous ethnic groups also have their own languages, but these languages are becoming increasingly marginalized. Vietnamese is still spoken by ethnic Vietnamese in Cambodia, and the Chinese dialects of Mandarin and Teochew are spoken by Chinese residing in the country.

Khmer verbs do not change depending on the time of the action. Instead of saying, "I ate," you would say, "I eat yesterday" in Khmer.

MINORITY LANGUAGES AND CONFLICT

The Khmer language is not only spoken in Cambodia: there are substantial numbers of Khmer people in other countries. As of 2016, more than one million Khmer live in the northeast of Thailand, and 1.4 million live in Vietnam (primarily in the Mekong Delta that was once part of the Khmer Empire). It is often difficult for minority communities to preserve their own language, especially when governments often see such attempts as a rejection of the majority culture. Recently, this has been the case in Vietnam. In Vietnam, public schooling is conducted almost entirely in Vietnamese, even in Khmer communities. This means the Khmer people of Vietnam are usually illiterate and unable to read or write their native language. This in turn leads to less economic opportunity. In 2008, protests were staged by Khmer monks in Vietnam over the treatment of their communities, but rather than addressing their concerns the Vietnamese government instituted a crackdown on dissent and forcibly defrocked a number of Khmer monks. The presence of minority languages often creates problems for an education system even with the best of intentions—it is more difficult to learn to read and write in a second language rather than one's first language. In Cambodia, too, the highest illiteracy rates are in communities of indigenous peoples.

FOREIGN INFLUENCES

Instead of saying, "How are you?" Cambodians say, "Have you eaten?"

For as long as Cambodia remained a French colony, the language of government and education was French. Even after the French left, there remained a tradition of speaking French among the urban elite. Fluency in the European language was a way for upper-class Cambodians to distinguish themselves from the majority. Even today, it is not unusual to come across educated Cambodians over the age of fifty who are fluent in French.

During the 1960s, partly due to the growing American influence in the affairs of the country, English began to supplant French. Both languages were still spoken by the educated elite when Pol Pot's army took control of the country in 1975. At that time, both French and English were regarded as signs of a decadent and corrupt lifestyle; anyone speaking either language was liable to be executed.

Such prohibitions were removed by the Vietnamese in 1978, but there was little need to speak any language except Khmer in the early years of reconstruction and renewal. Over the last twenty years or so, with the opening up of the country to development through foreign investment, there has been an explosion of interest in learning English. There is little interest in returning to French because French is not the language of international commerce. Instead, Phnom Penh has become a mecca for any Cambodian wanting to learn English. Increasingly, English fluency has become associated with economic progress.

There are now a number of English-language newspapers and magazines, although not all are published regularly. English newspapers include the *Phnom Penh Post* and the *Cambodia Times*.

INTERNET LINKS

www.britannica.com/topic/Austroasiatic-languages#ref604332
The Encyclopedia Britannica's website provides information about the entire Austroasiatic language family, which includes Khmer and Cham.

www.justlanded.com/english/Cambodia/Cambodia-Guide/Language/Languages-in-Cambodia
This site describes the different languages that are used in Cambodia and features a chart of letters in the Khmer alphabet with their equivalents in the Roman alphabet.

www.omniglot.com/language/phrases/khmer.php
Omniglot gives the translation of key phrases from English to Khmer.

ARTS

King Jayavarman VII is responsible for the splendor of Angkor Thom.

10

THE ARTS HAVE A LONG, ESTEEMED history in Cambodia. When most people think of Cambodian art, they imagine the spectacular architecture of Angkor Wat—the majestic towers and compelling sculptures carved into the temple walls. They might also think of the Royal Ballet of Cambodia, the dancers dressed in ornate costumes acting out stories that were first told centuries ago. But there is more to Cambodian art than this long history of traditional art forms. While these historical art forms are still treasured in present-day Cambodia, there is also a new and vibrant art scene in the country. Since the devastation of the Khmer Rouge, generations of Cambodian artists have arisen.

Henri Mouhot once declared that Angkor was "grander than anything of Greece or Rome."

STUNNING ARCHITECTURE

Some of the richest and most enduring aspects of Cambodian culture are found in the country's ancient architecture. The architecture of Angkor is the most famous example and is so powerful an artistic legacy that the Khmer Rouge used it to rationalize their policies.

"If our people can build Angkor Wat, they can do anything," announced Pol Pot in 1979. Ironically, the Khmer Rouge then set about destroying the country's cultural traditions; anyone with any connection with the world of art was ruthlessly murdered.

The complex of temples and royal buildings at Angkor—built entirely of stone and brick—is the supreme achievement of Cambodian art. Most of the temples were not built to house worshippers, unlike Christian or Muslim religious buildings. The Khmers walked around outside or gathered for prayers in wooden buildings that were erected separately. The existing buildings of Angkor were never intended for occupation by humans, but only for use as religious shrines. Only the gods were permitted to live in buildings of stone or brick. The remains of various wooden buildings have been discovered close to the *wats* (temples). These were the homes that made up the city of Angkor.

Most of the temples were built as acts of devotion to the Hindu god Vishnu. Building work culminated with Jayavarman VII, who built the Angkor Thom complex. For centuries, at the height of the Angkor civilization, each Khmer king strove to outdo his predecessor in the height, size, and splendor of his temples, culminating in the massive structures of Angkor Wat and the Bayon.

ANGKOR THOM The walled capital of Jayavarman VII was immense. It was surrounded by a moat 325 feet (100 m) wide, in addition to a stone wall 26 feet (8 m) high, with four imposing gateways that led to the Bayon. The Bayon was a pyramid temple with a tower 150 feet (46 m) high, with four huge carved heads at the top, facing the four compass points.

Encircling the main tower were fifty-one smaller towers with heads pointing in various directions. When a French writer first visited Angkor in 1912, he described the shattering effect of discovering this sight: "I looked

Angkor Thom's
Bayon temple

up at the tree-covered towers which dwarfed me, when all of a sudden my blood curdled as I saw an enormous smile looking down on me, and then another smile on another wall, then three, then five, then 10, appearing in every direction."

There are conflicting theories about the religious significance of Angkor Thom's architecture. The sculptures have been variously interpreted as representing the Buddha, Brahma, Shiva, and King Jayavarman himself.

ANGKOR WAT Angkor Wat is the best-known temple of the complex. According to legend, Angkor Wat was built by Indra, the Lord of Heaven, who came down to earth. Historically, however, King Suryavarman II was the ruler who began the building program. A number of monarchs then followed his example.

Angkor Wat measures about 2,800 by 3,300 feet (853 by 1,000 m) and contains a number of walled courtyards that encircle a central, five-towered building. The structure was built to represent Mount Meru, the sacred mountain regarded as the center of the world in the Hindu religion. The five towers symbolize the five peaks, the surrounding walls are the mountains, and the moat is the ocean at the end of the world.

The temple area is enclosed by a square moat, which is more than 3 miles (5 km) around. The adjoining wall is famous for its carvings and four monumental gateways. The large ground area is divided by long stone paths that are linked by the four gates.

The gates, in turn, lead to the inner sanctum, which contains a representation of Vishnu, to whom the wat was dedicated. The most ceremonial of the gateways faces westward, and the approaching stoneway is decorated with *naga* (nah-GAH), or snake, balustrades (low railings). On each side of the balustrades are two separate buildings, which are thought to have housed the capital's library of books and court documents.

TA PROHM Built as a Buddhist temple during the twelfth century, Ta Prohm is one of the largest Khmer buildings of the Angkor era. It is different from both Angkor Wat and Angkor Thom in that it has been left as it was found over a century ago by French archaeologists.

Here, more than at any other Angkor site, the work of nature has literally woven its way into the artistic stonework. Roots of massive trees have grown into and under the stone, and jungle growth is found everywhere. The result is what many consider a completely novel work of art—one that integrates the unrehearsed world of nature and the artificially crafted world of art.

THE EXCAVATION OF THE ANCIENT CITY

Angkor was deserted around 1430 when the monarchy moved farther south for security reasons. Angkor Wat gradually fell into disrepair, though it was used as a Buddhist pilgrimage center for some time. Some four hundred years later, French archaeologists began to excavate the site. The story begins with Henri Mouhot, a French naturalist who accidentally came across the ruins in the early 1860s. They were mostly covered in overgrown vegetation. The local inhabitants did not think it possible that their ancestors could ever have built such an astonishing temple complex. They told Mouhot that a race of giant gods had constructed the site.

A SNAPSHOT OF ANCIENT LIFE

Bas-reliefs cover huge sections of walls in Angkor Thom. A bas-relief is a sculpture or carving in which the figures project outward from the background. The bas-reliefs of Angkor make up the most impressive carvings of the temple complex. They usually illustrate figures and stories from the Ramayana *and other Hindu classics.*

What fascinates scholars and tourists about the bas-reliefs is the unique window they open on aspects of life in Khmer society. Examples of the type of armor and weapons used by the military are preserved in stone. So, too, are peaceful scenes of citizens shopping in the market, gambling at staged cockfights, or fishing in a river. Many of the scenes preserved in the bas-reliefs are still enacted in modern Cambodia, as well as in many other communities around the world. In many ways, gender roles have remained unchanged over the intervening centuries: young men are seen setting off in small groups on hunting trips, while their female peers visit hairdressers.

Angkor Thom's bas-reliefs have a story to tell.

Roots have caused substantial damage to Angkor Wat.

Serious restoration work began in the early 1990s. When Mouhot found the site, it had been left to nature for centuries and strangler figs had already caused damage. Roots and vines, having found their way into small cracks, had grown and split walls open. Today, there is some debate about the extent to which this kind of damage should be interfered with.

The long period of neglect allowed profiteers to plunder some of the statues. They were smuggled out of the country and sold to private art collectors around the world. The Khmer Rouge, for example, dismembered some of the statues and sold off the parts for revenue. As a result, a number of the statues that can be seen today in Angkor are decapitated.

PHNOM PENH'S SILVER PAGODA

The Silver Pagoda in Phnom Penh was preserved by the Khmer Rouge, although over half of the pagoda's contents were looted by the army. Despite the pillage, the extraordinary overall effect remains undiminished.

MOTIFS IN KHMER SCULPTURE

The asparas (as-PAH-rahs) represent the Angkor ideal of female beauty. They lived in heaven, where they were consorts of Khmer heroes and played an intercessory role between mortals and heaven. Asparas are nearly always portrayed wearing fine jewelry. The heads of the asparas have, unfortunately, become one of the most sought-after pieces of Angkor sculpture on the international art black market. A large number of them have disappeared since 1975.

Nagas are sacred snakes, guardians of water supplies, and they date back to Hindu mythology. The word naga is Sanskrit for "snake." In Hindu myths, the naga coils beneath Vishnu on the cosmic ocean. Khmer artists drew upon these myths

as material for their architectural designs. At Angkor, they are often found on stone balustrades.

The garuda (gah-ROO-dah) is a mythical half-man and half-bird creature. Traditionally, it is the enemy of the nagas. For unknown reasons, it appears later in Khmer architecture than any other motif.

Singhas (SING-ngahs) are lions that feature in Angkor architecture as guardians of temples. The singhas' characteristic lack of realistic features has been attributed to the fact that the sculptors had probably never seen real lions.

The Silver Pagoda

The pagoda is named for the silver tiles that make up the floor. The main staircase that leads up to the pagoda is made out of Italian marble. Inside, on a dais, a golden Buddha is seated. The Buddha contains nearly ten thousand diamonds and weighs about 200 pounds (91 kilograms). Flanking the golden Buddha are two smaller Buddhas, one bronze and one silver. Behind the golden figure sits another Buddha—made of marble—and a golden litter used to carry the king on coronation day. Twelve people are needed to carry the litter.

The pagoda's interior walls are decorated with priceless examples of Khmer art, including over twenty small gold Buddhas and crafted masks covered with jewels that were used by court dancers. A huge mural depicts scenes from the *Ramayana*.

SCULPTURE

Sculpture is a characteristic Cambodian art form. Although the most famous examples are those found at Angkor Wat, the history of Cambodian sculpture

THE ROYAL BALLET OF CAMBODIA

A Royal Ballet of Cambodia corps member dances Khmer classical choreography.

In 2008, the Royal Ballet of Cambodia was inscribed on the list of Intangible Cultural Heritage by UNESCO (United Nations Educational, Scientific and Cultural Organization). Intangible cultural history includes performance arts as well as things like food and digital history. The inclusion of the Royal Ballet of Cambodia is a recognition of the great value of this art form and its long tradition. The following description by UNESCO explains why it was inscribed on the list:

Renowned for its graceful hand gestures and stunning costumes, the Royal Ballet of Cambodia, also known as Khmer Classical Dance, has been closely associated with the Khmer court for over one thousand years. Performances would traditionally accompany royal ceremonies and observances such as coronations, marriages, funerals or Khmer holidays. This art form, which narrowly escaped annihilation in the 1970s, is cherished by many Cambodians. Infused with a sacred and symbolic role, the dance embodies the traditional values of refinement, respect and spirituality. Its repertory perpetuates the legends associated with the origins of the Khmer people. Consequently, Cambodians have long esteemed this tradition as the emblem of Khmer culture.

goes back to pre-Angkorian times. The National Museum of Art in Phnom Penh is the main repository for the country's stone masterpieces, including rare examples from the Funan period—beginning in the fourth century—as well as the Angkor and post-Angkor periods. Most of the art that predates the Angkorian period is Hindu-inspired. Angkor sculpture, which represents the supreme achievement of Khmer art and architecture, goes beyond the Hindu influence and blends motifs and techniques from Javanese art and Champa architecture.

One of the remarkable features of classical Khmer sculpture is its ability to represent realistic facial details. A stone face from the tenth century is recognizably that of a contemporary Cambodian, while at the same time conveying a religious sense of serenity and philosophic calm.

Khmer power peaked in the twelfth century when Angkor Wat was erected. The temples and their sculptures are a permanent testimony to Cambodia's powerful influence in Southeast Asia.

TRADITIONAL DANCES

The history of Cambodian dance goes back one thousand years, with its origins in the Indian influence on the royal courts. The courts shaped and encouraged this cultural tradition. The form of the dance is characterized by extremely detailed attention to the most minute movements of the dancer. The exact angle at which an elbow is pointed or a head tilted is all-important to the overall meaning of the spectacle.

Women perform the main roles in the court dance, including all the male characters. The only exception is the character of the monkey, which is always played by a man.

Some members of the national dance troupe who escaped the Khmer Rouge fled to the United States, where they kept alive their classic art form. Through years of effort by a small group of dancers who believe that this dance is a vital part of Cambodia's national identity, this art has been revived. While holding onto the traditions of the dance, stories and themes have been reinvented to reflect political and social changes in present-day Cambodia.

One of the survivors of the Khmer Rouge was Chleng Phong, who later became a minister of culture. He speaks endearingly of his country's dance: "For me, the classical Cambodian dance is the perfection of human artistic expression." The passion that Cambodians have for their dance is reflected in their persistence in the art despite all obstacles.

FOLK DANCE There is a difference between court dancing and folk dancing. Court dancing is highly formalized and akin to ballet in some respects. The dancers practice long hours and strive to perfect classic movements and postures. Folk dancing is less formally structured and allows for improvisation arising from the interplay between the group of musicians and the team of dancers. Drums are usually used to establish a leading rhythm, and the dancers then weave their movements around this rhythm. However, in the 1960s, under Sihanouk, a number of folk dances were also codified and stylized and entered the canon of Khmer dance together with court dances.

The more flexible and improvisational nature of folk dancing helps explain how it managed to survive the cultural nihilism of the Pol Pot regime. Court dancers were a relatively small group of professional, elite dancers who were singled out for persecution by the Khmer Rouge. Being based in Phnom Penh made them especially vulnerable. Members of folk dance troupes were more likely to live in rural areas, and because they had a rural background, they were less likely to be identified as enemies of the new regime.

LITERATURE

Cambodian literature has two great epics: the *Poem of Angkor Wat*, from the early seventeenth century, and the *Ramakerti*, which dates from between the sixteenth and mid-eighteenth centuries and has its origins in the seminal Indian epic the *Ramayana*. The subject matter of the *Ramayana*—the life of Rama—also occurs in Cambodian dance-dramas and sculpture, a testimony to the influence of Indian art on Southeast Asia. The epics were oral in nature and depended for their success on storytelling sessions by professional groups who recited the tales.

The *Poem of Angkor Wat*, carved into its walls in the sixteenth century, credits the gods with the temple's construction.

WITNESS TO GENOCIDE

In 2011, the famed Cambodian painter and artist Vann Nath died at the age of sixty-five. He was one of only seven people to survive his stay at notorious Khmer Rouge prison Tuol Sleng, where over twelve thousand Cambodians were tortured and killed. Vann Nath was spared from execution in order to paint portraits of Pol Pot. After the genocide ended, Vann Nath bore witness to the crimes of the regime. He painted the scenes he saw in prison: inmates being tortured in different ways and mass executions. He later testified at the trial of Kang Kek Iew, the warden of the prison. His paintings and testimony are an important source of information about the crimes that were committed by the Khmer Rouge. Yet Vann Nath did more than paint scenes from prison. He also painted pastoral scenes from his childhood as well as less realistic paintings rich in symbolism and myth. Later in life, he was involved in a documentary where he was reunited with his former prison guards and torturers so that he could confront them about their actions. Vann Nath's works and life of dignity are a tribute to the many victims who were silenced by the genocidal regime of the Khmer Rouge.

Folk stories have figured in Cambodian culture throughout recorded history. From about the eighteenth century, this populist tradition began to be supplemented by verse fiction. A common inspiration was the Jataka, the various stories of previous lives of the Buddha. The most popular of these recounts the story of Prince Vesandar, an example of supreme charity and generosity, who was willing to give away all his possessions, even his wife and children.

During French colonial rule, printing was introduced to Cambodia and acted as the catalyst for the development of new literary forms. The first modern novel to be written in prose, as opposed to the usual verse form, was *Suphat*. It was written by Rim Kin (1911—1959) and was published in the year 1938.

Under Pol Pot, literature ceased to have any meaningful role in the cultural life of the country. Books, both fiction and nonfiction, were destroyed as a matter of principle, and any display of literary knowledge or interest was regarded as a form of heresy.

Present developments in the economic and social life of the country are likely to lead to a renewal of interest in the country's literary heritage. However, the explosion of interest in the English language may undermine conventional Cambodian literary forms.

INTERNET LINKS

www.cambodiamuseum.info
The National Museum of Cambodia's website has a description of Khmer art history as well as descriptions and pictures of recent exhibitions.

www.nga.gov/exhibitions/cambodia/camrm2a-1.htm
The National Gallery of Art in Washington, DC, provides a virtual tour of its Cambodian exhibit online.

www.unesco.org/culture/ich/en/RL/royal-ballet-of-cambodia-00060
UNESCO's website describes the Royal Ballet of Cambodia and includes a video of a performance.

LEISURE

Free time in Cambodia is often spent socializing with family and friends.

11

LIKE WESTERNERS, CAMBODIANS enjoy passing the time chatting, eating, and drinking with friends and family. Using smartphones to play games and connect with others via social media is also rapidly becoming more and more popular. On the other hand, expensive leisure activities like traveling are still out of reach for most Cambodians. Furthermore, the fact that most Cambodians live outside of cities rules out many leisure activities that we are most familiar with, such as going to movie theaters or shopping malls.

Among remote indigenous peoples, pipe smoking is a popular pastime, especially among young women.

SPECIAL SOJOURNS

A visit to a temple for a festival is a popular leisure activity. It is an occasion for a family to put on their best clothes. If the festival is a particularly important one, the family may have saved some money to get cloth to make new clothes.

The Water Festival in Phnom Penh is an especially popular event. People from outside the capital use the occasion to make a visit to the city and meet friends and relatives.

Fireworks are part of Phnom Penh's Water Festival.

The capital city offers the promise of work, and many young Cambodians have left their villages and traveled long distances in the hope of finding employment in Phnom Penh. The Water Festival represents an occasion for rural families to visit their sons or daughters in the big city.

In the past, a traditional form of entertainment in the countryside was provided by traveling troupes of dancers, who were hired to perform at a local festival or a wedding. Local dance troupes often presented classic stories taken from Hindu epics like the *Ramayana*, with easily recognizable character types such as the beautiful princess or the intolerant father. Led by the National Dance Company, these dances have now been revived.

URBAN RECREATION

The only place in Cambodia where neon lights advertise the kind of leisure activities and services familiar to most Westerners—movie theaters, restaurants, night clubs—is the capital city of Phnom Penh. Watching movies has always been a popular pastime with city dwellers, not least because the price of a ticket is affordable.

Cambodians are most likely to spend their evenings talking over the day's events with friends and neighbors. A friendly conversation is considered a worthwhile activity in itself, and the local storyteller is always a valued member of any community.

Even in Phnom Penh, where the impact of technology is growing, most people still conduct their lives at a leisurely pace. Most offices and shops close for at least an hour (and often twice as long) for lunch. Cambodians enjoy socializing with friends and neighbors, and their strong work ethic does not prevent them from seeking other people's company.

Today, around 90 percent of Cambodians report having access to a television and radio, although the rate of ownership is much lower. In the countryside, radios are more common. Folk plays and shadow plays have made a comeback, reclaiming the following they once had in farming communities on festive occasions. The figures that are used in shadow plays are usually cut out of leather and painted in an exaggerated style to convey the characters' distinct personalities.

Gambling has traditionally been a popular male pastime, although there are no official betting shops or state lotteries in Cambodia.

Central Market is Cambodia's biggest market.

POPULAR DANCE

Dance is a popular form of aerobic exercise in Cambodia.

Dance plays a large part in Cambodian culture. It is a necessity during festivals, weddings, celebrations, ancestral worship, or as part of a theatrical performance. Apart from the highly stylized court dances, Cambodians also dance socially. Ramkbach and Ramvong are popular social dances. Participants do not dance with partners but in a circle. The focus is on the graceful movement of the hands.

SPORTS

The Cambodia National Soccer Team plays international matches, but it has yet to qualify for the World Cup.

Since the fall of the Khmer Rouge and the opening of Cambodia to the rest of the world, sports have become more popular in Cambodia. Like across much of the world, soccer is the most popular sport both for young people to play and for adults to watch. Many other sports that are specific to Cambodia and Southeast Asia are also popular. For example, *sepak takraw* is played in

Cambodia and across the region. This sport resembles volleyball, but hitting the ball with one's hands is forbidden. Players use their other body parts, especially their feet and heads, to knock the ball over a net.

A number of martial arts also exist in Cambodia that were practiced in ancient times and have been preserved to this day. Khmer traditional wrestling and *pradal serey*, a type of martial art that involves both kicking and punching, appear in bas-reliefs and are still popular forms of recreation.

Traditional wrestling plays a part in some festivals, like the Pchum Ben festival shown here.

INTERNET LINKS

www.bokatorcambodia.com
Bokator, a Cambodian martial art, is featured on this website that includes some videos and pictures of the sport in action.

realworldrecords.com/artist/546/musicians-of-the-national-dance-company-of-cambodia
This website features a short history of music and dance in Cambodia in addition to samples of Cambodian songs you can listen to.

www.sepaktakraw.org/about-istaf/how-to-play-the-game
The official website of sepak takraw explains the rules of the game and includes a video of some gameplay.

FESTIVALS

The Water Festival includes dragon boat races.

THERE ARE NUMEROUS FESTIVALS and public holidays in Cambodia. In 2016, there were nineteen public holidays that took place over twenty-eight days throughout the year! Many of these public holidays in Cambodia are religious in nature. They often involve going to the local temple and donating food or money to the monks there. Other holidays simply relate to Cambodian history; for instance, the king's birthday is a holiday, as is the day Cambodia achieved independence from France. Still others, like Labor Day and Children's Day, are international holidays that are observed in Cambodia.

12

With different calendars for measuring time in Cambodia, confusion is always a possibility. Therefore, the Buddhist day, month, or year often appears alongside the Western date in announcements.

CHANGING DATES

The dates of most festivals in Cambodia are determined according to the Khmer lunar calendar. Thus, the actual dates of festivals vary slightly from one year to the next.

The Western calendar is used by the government and the business community, but when it comes to calculating the time of a festival, a

Revelers celebrate Cambodian New Year in Siem Reap

more traditional calendar is employed. This calendar is of Indian origin and is basically lunar, although various corrections are periodically introduced to bring it in line with the solar yearly cycle.

Buddhist festivals are calculated according to the lunar calendar, which begins in the month of November or December. The Cambodian New Year's Day, however, is based on solar calculations and is celebrated in April. The traditional calendar divides the twelve months, alternately, into male and female ones. According to tradition, a wedding festival should take place only during the female months. Each month is divided in half and the days are numbered 1 to 15 or 1 to 14 (months have either 29 or 30 days). The first half of any month, when the moon is waxing, has the word *kaoet* (COW-er)—meaning to be born—added to the number. The second half of a month is indicated by adding the word *roc* (raw)—meaning to grow less.

By tradition, certain days of the week are considered more auspicious than others. Saturday, for instance, is deemed a day when unhelpful spirits are allowed to wander the earth, and Cambodians avoid holding local temple festivals on that day. Such beliefs, however, are more likely to be found among older people, especially those living in remote rural areas. The average Cambodian living in Phnom Penh would prefer that a festival not be held on a Saturday simply because it is another working day.

KHMER NEW YEAR

The Cambodian New Year marks the start of the most lively festival period across the whole country. It lasts at least three days and is one of the few times of the year when the majority of Cambodians take time off from work. On the last day of the old year, houses are traditionally cleaned from top to bottom and everything is made presentable for the New Year.

Aligned around the monsoon season, the Rains Retreat, sometimes called Buddhist lent, is a three-month period when monks remain in one place and lay followers sometimes give up luxuries such as smoking or eating meat.

CALENDAR OF FESTIVALS

April

Chaul Chnam is the name of a three-day festival that usually occurs around the middle of the month. It is an important event and marks the beginning of the Cambodian New Year.

Visak Bochea occurs later in the month (or in May) and is a commemoration of the birth and enlightenment of the Buddha.

May

Royal Ploughing Ceremony is an agricultural festival that marks the beginning of the rice-sowing season.

September

Pchum Ben occurs toward the end of the month (or in October) and marks a time when villagers pay homage to their ancestors. This is a ritual of Hindu origin and serves as a reminder of the influence of non-Buddhist spirit worship that can still be found across Cambodia.

The festival is conducted mainly through monasteries, with people bringing offerings in the mornings. During the evenings, talks and sermons are given by some of the monks.

Over a period of fifteen days, people make offerings of balls of rice to their ancestors. It is believed that the king of the Land of the Dead permits spirits to visit their relatives on earth during this period. On the last day, the 15th, Cambodians make a special effort to be in the village where the ashes of their closest relatives rest. Special cakes are prepared and offered to the local temple.

October/November

The Water Festival is also known as the Festival of the Reversing Current. As the second name suggests, this festival marks the moment when the Tonle Sap River reverses its flow. The Tonle Sap lake fills with the floodwaters of the Mekong for five to six months. The Water Festival commemorates the emptying of the lake water back into the Mekong.

January/February

Tet marks the Vietnamese and Chinese New Year and is celebrated by the ethnic Vietnamese and Chinese citizens of Cambodia. It is essentially a family event and has some similarities to Thanksgiving in the United States and Canada. It is a time to gather with one's family members in a spirit of joy and participate in celebratory meals.

On New Year's Day, many Cambodians pay a family visit to their local temple and pray for a good future. Another tradition, though no longer common, is the making of small sand hillocks around the temple grounds and inserting little homemade paper flags in them.

Children use the holiday to fly their kites. The kites, which are made by the children themselves, are carefully crafted out of spare cloth and trimmed pieces of bamboo. Vegetable dyes are used to paint geometric designs or colorful animal shapes on the cloth.

Fireworks, usually imported from China, also form part of the New Year celebrations.

THE ORDINATION CEREMONY

The beginning of the rainy season is the traditional time for the ordination of monks and novices. The ceremonies, though highly ritualized, are colorful social occasions. The young novices form a procession that winds its way around the ordination area three times. The procession also includes a number of monks whose chanting provides the musical background to the ritual. Parents, friends, and relatives are understandably proud of the young men who are about to enter temple life, and they show up in their best clothes to witness the event.

BANNING FESTIVALS

Under Pol Pot, most of the traditional festivals were strictly outlawed. All festivals were fiercely rejected by the Khmer Rouge because they were often religious in nature and some of them were associated with royalty.

For example, the agricultural festival that celebrates the beginning of the sowing season in May used to include a member of the royal family ritually plowing the first furrow of the year. The Water Festival involved a member of royalty officially commanding the waters of the Tonle Sap River to change their direction.

THE CAMBODIAN FILM FESTIVAL

In addition to traditional and religious festivals, there are also modern festivals in Cambodia. One such festival is the Cambodian International Film Festival (CIFF), which has taken place every year since 2010 in Phnom Penh. The CIFF lasts for six days and showcases Cambodian movies and foreign movies about Cambodia, as well as other interesting films. In 2015, more than eighty films from thirty-four different countries were shown in more than two hundred viewings. Audiences are composed of both Cambodians and foreigners, but according to the festival programmer, one of the main goals of the CIFF is to encourage Cambodians to go to the theater.

In 2015, the CIFF came into the international spotlight with the involvement of American actress Angelina Jolie. She became the president of the CIFF's honorary committee and helped to raise awareness about the event. In a statement, she said:

> I'm really looking forward to participating in the festival, and meeting artists whose work I so admire. I am having a wonderful experience working with talented Cambodian artists like Rithy Panh, who is producing the film [*First They Killed My Father*] with me. Cambodia is a great home for art and creativity, with a rich culture and promising future, and I think that is what everyone will see at this year's festival.

INTERNET LINKS

www.bodhikaram.com/Pchum%20Ben.html
The website of a Khmer Buddhist monastery explains the significance of the Pchum Ben festival.

cambodia-iff.com/index.php/en
The official website of the Cambodian International Film Festival details the films that are shown for the current year.

www.mef.gov.kh/public-holiday.html
The Cambodian Ministry of Economy and Finance gives the dates for all public holidays.

International Children's Day is celebrated on June 1 in Cambodia.

FOOD

Kuy teav

13

C AMBODIAN CUISINE IS RENOWNED for its complex flavors and rich variety of spices. It uses a large number of different pastes, sauces, and spices that can be salty, sour, pungent, sweet, and hot—sometimes all in the same dish! The most important foods are undoubtedly rice and fish, but these seemingly simple ingredients are used to create a wide array of very different dishes.

In many ways, Cambodian cuisine is very similar to that of neighboring countries such as Vietnam. Many of the same spices and ingredients are used in both countries due to their close proximity and similar climate and environment. Some of the most popular Cambodian street food would be quite at home in Singapore or Thailand. Yet Cambodian cuisine has its own unique qualities that sometimes make it quite different from its neighbors. For instance, the fish paste *prahok* is found only in Cambodia—a fact that Cambodians are quite proud of.

RICE, A STAPLE FOOD

Sii bay (SEE-bay)—the Cambodian verb that means "to eat"—becomes "to eat rice" when translated literally. This is testimony to the importance of rice in the Cambodian diet. Only in exceptional circumstances would someone go through a day without having a meal that includes rice.

Black Sticky Rice 흑미

Many varieties of rice are used in Cambodian cooking.

It is the primary carbohydrate and energy source for Cambodians. The Cambodian liking for rice is not unusual in Southeast Asia. Their neighbors, the Vietnamese, Thais, and Laotians, share this dietary dependence.

Rice is not the only feature of Cambodian food common to Southeast Asia. Many of the herbs and spices used to flavor dishes are found throughout the region. There is also a liking for the hot and sour tastes characteristic of Thai cooking.

The typical dish that accompanies a bowl of rice is fish. A fish-based soup is also commonly consumed with a meal but is not regarded as a separate dish that precedes the main meal. It is dipped into when the rice and fish are being eaten and helps to balance the dryness of the rice.

Meat, when available, is also eaten with rice. Chicken is the most common, followed by beef and pork. Wild game is not commonly available in urban areas, but in the countryside villagers like to supplement their diet with protein-rich wild boar meat or large birds.

A rice-based dish that is especially popular with Cambodians is called *ansom chek* (an-sam-KRU). This meal is made by mixing tiny pieces of cooked

pork with tofu and rolling the mixture in rice. Legend has it that a meatless version of ansom chek was a personal favorite of the Buddha himself.

Vendors at Kep Market sell barbecued fish of all kinds.

DRIED AND FRESH FISH

Like rice, fish dominates the typical Cambodian meal. Depending on the season and location, Cambodians eat either fresh fish or salted, dried fish. Freshwater fish is caught mostly from the Tonle Sap or the Mekong River. In recent years, however, the destruction of forests in many lowland central provinces has also disrupted or destroyed the rivers in those forests that are the natural breeding habitats of many species of freshwater fish.

When fresh fish is available, most Cambodians prefer to grill rather than boil or bake it. A traditional method of presenting food on a plate is to cut the grilled fish into small pieces and wrap them in leaves of lettuce or spinach. Additional flavor is provided by a fish sauce called *tuk trey* (TOUK-tra).

SPICING IT UP

Fermented fish sauce, tuk trey, is the most characteristic condiment in Cambodia. It has a distinctive odor, which those who are unused to the smell often find difficult to appreciate. Tuk trey is made by fermenting salted fish in large pots for at least three months. This condiment is also found in Vietnam, but the Cambodian version is distinguished by the addition of ground peanuts.

Cambodian salads are different from those in the United States or Europe. They usually contain some meat, if available, and are flavored with herbs such as lemon grass, mint, and coriander. The result is a hot, spicy taste that has little in common with the typical lightly dressed salad of Western dinner tables.

Dried fish and rice—whether steamed, boiled, or fried—can become monotonously familiar and nondescript to the taste buds. Cambodians often enliven the taste of the basic ingredients with chilies and garlic. Various herbs are also added whenever they are available.

Lemongrass is an important ingredient in Cambodian cuisine.

DELICACIES

On special occasions, such as a wedding or an important festival like the New Year, the usual rice and dried fish meal gives way to something more elaborate. Fresh shrimp barbecued over a small open fire is a particular favorite with many Cambodians. So, too, are roasted sunflower seeds. Other delicacies include duck eggs, known as *pong tea kon* (PONG-tee-ko), which are eaten just before they are ready to hatch, and fried crunchy cicadas, known as *chong roet* (CHONG-rot).

Another specialty consists of pieces of banana wrapped inside balls of sticky rice. A favorite dessert for special occasions is a pudding known as *sangkcha khnor* (SANK-cha kor), which is made from jackfruit.

One of the most important foods in Cambodia is prahok—a kind of fermented fish paste. Prahok has a strong, distinct taste that is difficult to describe. It is eaten both as a food and used as an ingredient to flavor soups and sauces. Due to its high protein content, it is an important part of the traditional Cambodian diet.

Every winter, fishermen around Cambodia catch tons of small fish that they use to make prahok. The fish are decapitated and the bodies are crushed underfoot or ground up by small machines. The resulting fish pulp is left to dry in the sun for a day before being mixed with salt and fermented in jars or bags for months. Farmers from inland travel to the fishing communities to trade rice for the nutritious prahok. But prahok prices have risen recently as the Tonle Sap is overfished, and some fear the food will become increasingly expensive and rare in the future.

These fish, caught in the Tonle Sap, will be used to make prahok.

For now, prahok remains one of the most typical Cambodian ingredients. According to government official Nao Thouk in an interview with journalist Suy Se, "Prahok is the taste of Cambodia. If there is no prahok, we are not Cambodians. Prahok is the Khmer identity. It is like butter or cheese for Westerners."

The French colonial era brought a different style of cooking to the country, and there is still some tangible evidence of this. French bread, for example, is very popular. French cuisine, however, never reached the vast majority of rural Cambodians; it is primarily in Phnom Penh that French culinary influence is seen. Frog legs are considered a local delicacy, but this predates the arrival of the French.

BEVERAGES

Cambodians enjoy drinking tea between—and often with—all their meals. Coffee is also drunk, either black or with condensed milk. A visitor to a Cambodian home is more likely to be offered a cup of tea than any other refreshment.

In drink stalls in towns and Phnom Penh, the most popular cool drink is soda water with fresh lemon. A large slice of lemon is often placed on a side plate and the customer squeezes the juice into the water. Well-known international brands of canned soft drinks have also begun to appear in the capital. Cambodians generally do not drink alcohol. But alcohol consumption has increased in recent years as it correlates to status and discretionary income.

SERVING THE MEAL

Rice, the basic component of any meal, is often placed on the table in a large serving bowl or plate. Diners then fills their smaller individual bowls, refilling them later if they wish. Depending on how large or elaborate the meal is, there are serving plates for the fish and other dishes, and smaller, saucer-like plates for the condiments.

Diners use their chopsticks to add a quantity of the fish, meat, or vegetables to their own bowl of rice. The bowl is typically held close to the mouth, and the food eaten with the chopsticks. It is not uncommon, in rural areas especially, for people to eat an informal meal using just their fingers instead of chopsticks.

Meals in Cambodia often include an array of dishes.

In Cambodian culture, chopstick placement is a part of good table manners.

When a meal is over, the chopsticks are placed across the bowl or just left by the side. Leaving the chopsticks sticking up out of the bowl is considered bad manners.

RICE AND THE KHMER ROUGE

The Battambang region has traditionally provided Cambodia with most of its rice. There was a time before the 1970s when Battambang provided all the rice that Cambodia needed, and the produce from other parts of the country could be exported. The fact that rice was the country's largest source of foreign exchange formed the basis for the economic policies of the Khmer Rouge, which emphasized the development of agriculture.

The Khmer Rouge planned to dramatically increase the country's rice production. The foreign currency earned would finance imports of farm machinery and fertilizer and thereby help make the country self-sufficient.

The government slogan was "three tons [of harvested rice] per hectare." This meant tripling the average yield throughout the country, with only four years allowed to achieve this miracle. The plan, however, ignored the facts: Cambodia was just emerging from five devastating years of war, and there was a shortage of tools, seed, and livestock.

What followed was a desperate attempt to meet unreasonable quotas. Towns and cities were emptied of their populations. The result was the deaths of hundreds of thousands of overworked and starving Cambodians. Today, Cambodia is still recovering from this traumatic period. The people of Cambodia remain among the poorest in Southeast Asia, and for many families, malnutrition is just one bad harvest away.

INTERNET LINKS

www.asian-recipe.com/cambodia
This website provides dozens of recipes as well as descriptions of typical Cambodian ingredients.

www.cambodia-hotels.com/food.htm
A variety of descriptions and pictures of Cambodian dishes are available at this travel website.

www.food.com/topic/cambodian
Food.com features a section of Cambodian recipes.

SHRIMP ROLLS

25 peeled and deveined raw shrimp
25 packaged pre-made spring roll shells
1 teaspoon of salt
A bottle of sunflower oil

Rinse the shrimp after thawing them (if they are frozen); toss the shrimp with the salt in a bowl. Place a shrimp in the corner of a spring roll shell and carefully wrap it in the shell. If the shell is too big, cut it in half and begin again. Once all the shrimp are wrapped, add enough oil to a pot to completely cover a shrimp roll. Preheat the oil on medium heat for a couple minutes; then carefully place shrimp rolls in the heated oil using tongs until the bottom of the pot is covered with rolls. Cook until they are light brown and crispy. Remove the shrimp rolls with tongs and begin cooking the next batch in the same oil.

LOK LAK (SAUTEED BEEF)

8 ounces cubed beef
3 tablespoons minced garlic
3 tablespoons soy sauce
½ teaspoon salt
1 tablespoon ketchup
1 tablespoon fish sauce
½ tablespoon sugar
3 tablespoons sunflower oil
1 cup chopped lettuce
1 slice of tomato
1 slice of red onion

Marinate the cubed beef in the minced garlic, soy sauce, and salt for 30 minutes. Prepare a bed of lettuce with slices of red onion and tomato on the side. Heat the oil in a frying pan on medium heat and then add the beef and a dash of the marinade; cook the beef, stirring frequently, until the outside is browned. Mix the ketchup, fish sauce, and sugar to make a sauce and add it to the cooked beef. When this mixture is warmed, place the beef on the bed of lettuce and drizzle some of the leftover sauce over the food.

THAILAND

LAOS

1

Dangrek

Mountains

Samrong

**BANTEAY
MEANCHEY**

PREAH VIHEAR

Tonle Kong

Se San

RATANAKIRI

Boung
Long

Poipet

Sisophon

SIEM REAP

Phnom Thbeng
Meanchey

STUNG TRENG

Srepok

■ *Angkor*

Siem Reap

Stung Sen

Stung Treng

Batdambang

Tonle

2

BATDAMBANG

Sap

KAMPONG THOM

KRATIE

MONDULKIRI

Kampong
Thom

Pursat

▲

*Phnom
Tumpor*

PURSAT

**KAMPONG
CHHNANG**

Kampong
Chhnang

▲

Kratie

Mekong

Semonorom

Cardamom Mountains

Phnom Aural
(5,949 ft / 1,813 m)

Kampong
Cham

**KAMPONG
CHAM**

N

3

**KAMPONG
SPEU**

Krong Koh Kong

*Prek
Thnot*

**PHNOM
PENH**

Ta
Khmau

Prey Veng

Kas Kong

KOH KONG

Kampong
Speu

KANDAL

**PREY
VENG**

**SVAY
RIENG**

Bay of Kampong Som

Elephant Mts

Takeo

Bassac

Svay
Rieng

Kas Rong

Kampong Som
(Sihanoukville)

KAMPOT

TAKEO

Kampot

VIETNAM

4

Gulf

of

Thailand

5

●	Capital city	
●	Major town	
▲	Mountain peak	
■	Ancient site	

Feet		Meters
16,500		5,000
9,900		3,000
6,600		2,000
3,300		1,000
1,650		500
660		200
0		0

MAP OF CAMBODIA

Angkor, B2

Banteay Meanchey, A1, A2

Bassac River, C3, C4

Batdambang City, A2

Batdambang Province, A2, A3, B2

Bay of Kampong Som, A4, B4

Boung Long, D1

Cardamom Mountains, B3, B4

Dangrek Mountains, B1, C1

Elephant Mountains, B3, B4

Kampong Cham City, C3

Kampong Cham Province, B3, C2, C3

Kampong Chhnang Province, B2, B3

Kampong Chhnang Town, B3

Kampong Som, B4

Kampong Speu Province, B3, B4

Kampong Speu Town, B3

Kampong Thom Province, B2, B3, C2, C3

Kampong Thom Town, B2

Kampot Province, B3, B4

Kampot Town, B4

Kandal, B3, B4, C3, C4

Kas Kong , A3

Kas Rong, A4

Koh Kong Province, A3, A4, B3, B4

Kratie Province, C2, C3, D2, D3

Kratie Town, C2

Krong Koh Kong, A3

Mekong River, C1, C2, C3, B3

Mondulkiri Province, C2, C3, D2, D3

Phnom Aural, B3

Phnom Penh City, B3

Phnom Thbeng Meanchey, B2

Phnom Tumpor, A3

Poipet, A2

Preah Vihear, B1, B2, C1, C2

Prek Thnot Lake, B3

Prey Veng Province, C3, C4

Prey Veng Town, C3

Pursat City, B2

Pursat Province, A2, A3, B2, B3

Ratanakiri, D1, D2

Samrong, B1

Samrong River, A2

Semonorom, D3

Se San River, D1

Siem Reap City, B2

Siem Reap Province, A1, A2, B1, B2

Sisophon, A2

Srepok River, D2

Stung Sen, C2

Stung Treng Province, C1, C2, D1, D2

Stung Treng Town, C2

Svay Rieng Province, C3, C4

Svay Rieng Town, C4

Ta Khmau, C3

Takeo Province, B3, B4, C4

Takeo Town, B4

Tonle Kong River, C1

Tonle Sap lake, B2, B3

Tonle Sap River, B3

ECONOMIC CAMBODIA

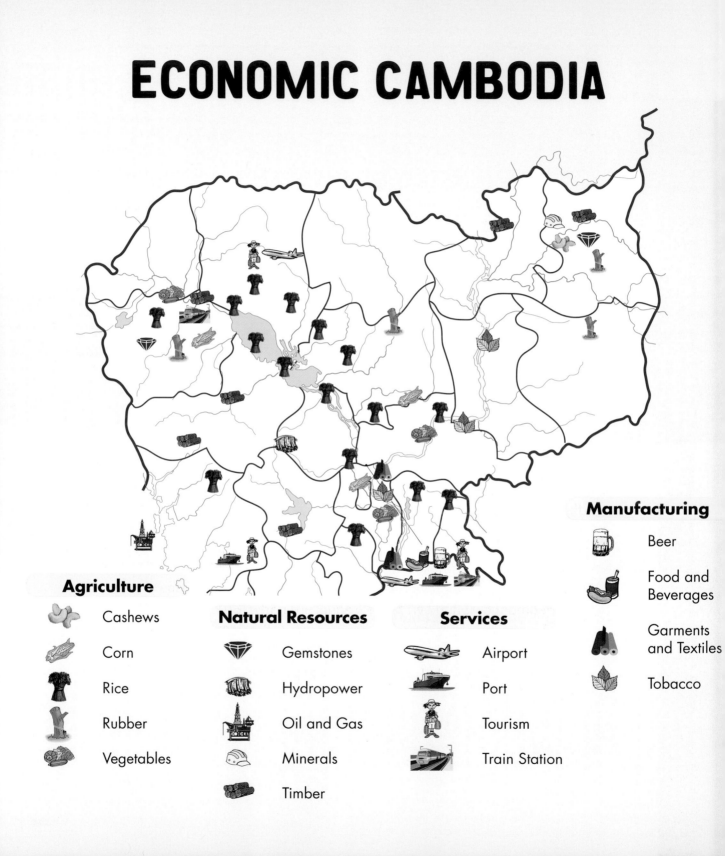

Agriculture
- Cashews
- Corn
- Rice
- Rubber
- Vegetables

Natural Resources
- Gemstones
- Hydropower
- Oil and Gas
- Minerals
- Timber

Services
- Airport
- Port
- Tourism
- Train Station

Manufacturing
- Beer
- Food and Beverages
- Garments and Textiles
- Tobacco

ABOUT THE ECONOMY

OVERVIEW

Still suffering from the effects of civil war and political instability, the economy of Cambodia remains small although it is one of the fastest growing in the world. Most Cambodians are employed in agriculture and light industry. However, the tourism industry is an area of great potential that the Cambodian government is seeking to expand.

GROSS DOMESTIC PRODUCT (GDP)

$18.16 billion (2015 estimate)

GDP GROWTH

6.9 percent (2015 estimate)

INFLATION RATE

1.2 percent (2015 estimate)

LAND USE

Arable land 22.7 percent; permanent crops 0.9 percent; other 76.4 percent (2005 estimates)

CURRENCY

Cambodian riel (KHR)
Notes: 50, 100, 200, 500, 1,000, 2,000, 5,000, 10,000, 20,000, 50,000, 100,000 riel
1 USD = 4,089 KHR (July 2016)

NATURAL RESOURCES

Oil and gas, timber, gemstones, iron ore, manganese, phosphates, hydropower potential, arable land

AGRICULTURAL PRODUCTS

Rice, rubber, corn, vegetables, cashews, tapioca

INDUSTRY

Tourism, garments, rice milling, fishing, wood and wood products, rubber, cement, gem mining, textiles

MAJOR EXPORTS

Rice, fish, timber, garments, rubber, tobacco (2015)

MAJOR IMPORTS

Petroleum products, construction materials, vehicles and motorcycles, clothing (2015)

MAIN TRADE PARTNERS

United States, United Kingdom, Germany, Japan, Canada, China, Vietnam, Thailand, the Netherlands (2015)

POPULATION BELOW POVERTY LINE

17.7 percent (2012 estimate)

WORKFORCE

7.97 million (2013 estimate)

UNEMPLOYMENT RATE

0.3 percent (2013 estimate)

EXTERNAL DEBT

$7.2 billion (2014 estimate)

CULTURAL CAMBODIA

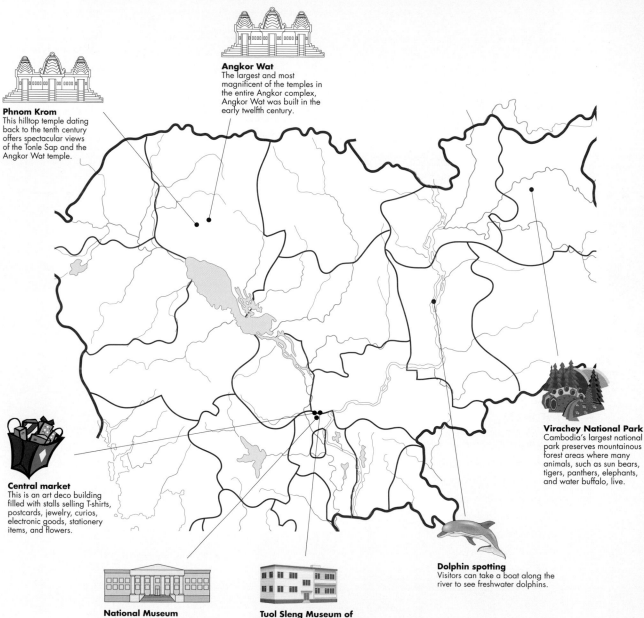

Angkor Wat
The largest and most magnificent of the temples in the entire Angkor complex, Angkor Wat was built in the early twelfth century.

Phnom Krom
This hilltop temple dating back to the tenth century offers spectacular views of the Tonle Sap and the Angkor Wat temple.

Central market
This is an art deco building filled with stalls selling T-shirts, postcards, jewelry, curios, electronic goods, stationery items, and flowers.

Virachey National Park
Cambodia's largest national park preserves mountainous forest areas where many animals, such as sun bears, tigers, panthers, elephants, and water buffalo, live.

Dolphin spotting
Visitors can take a boat along the river to see freshwater dolphins.

National Museum
Built in 1917, this museum houses an extensive collection of ancient Khmer artifacts from the pre- to post-Angkorian period.

Tuol Sleng Museum of Genocidal Crime
A school that was used as a prison during the Pol Pot era, this museum displays pictures of people who were killed and instruments of torture as a reminder of the genocide.

ABOUT THE CULTURE

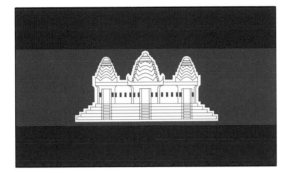

OFFICIAL NAME
Kingdom of Cambodia

FLAG DESCRIPTION
Three horizontal bands—blue, red, blue—with a white three-towered temple, representing Angkor Wat, in the center of the red band

CAPITAL
Phnom Penh

POPULATION
15.7 million (2015 estimate)

BIRTH RATE
23.8 births per 1,000 Cambodians (2015 estimate)

DEATH RATE
7.68 deaths per 1,000 Cambodians (2015 estimate)

AGE DISTRIBUTION
0 to 14 years: 31.4 percent; 15 to 64 years: 64.5 percent; 65 years and over: 4.1 percent (2015 estimates)

ETHNIC GROUPS
Khmer 90 percent, Vietnamese 5 percent, Chinese 1 percent, other 4 percent (2015 estimates)

RELIGIOUS GROUPS
Theravada Buddhist 96.9 percent, Muslim 1.9 percent, Christian 0.4 percent, other 0.8 percent (2008 estimates)

MAIN LANGUAGES
Khmer (official)

LITERACY RATE
77.2 percent (2015 estimate)

IMPORTANT HOLIDAYS
Victory Day (January 7); New Year (three days in April); Labor Day (May 1); Ancestors' Day (a day in September or October depending on the lunar calendar); Independence Day (November 9); Water Festival (three days in November also in accordance with the lunar calendar)

LEADERS IN POLITICS
Pol Pot—prime minister of Democratic Kampuchea (1976–1979)
Hun Sen—prime minister of People's Republic (1985–1989) and State of Cambodia (1989–1993); second prime minister (1993–1998); first prime minister (1998–)
Prince Norodom Ranariddh—first prime minister of State of Cambodia (1993) and under restored monarchy (1993–1997)

TIMELINE

IN CAMBODIA	IN THE WORLD
600 Khmer civilization is established.	**600** Height of Mayan civilization
802 Unified Khmer Empire is created.	
889 The capital is moved to Angkor.	
1113 Construction of Angkor Wat begins.	**1000** The Chinese perfect gunpowder and begin to use it in warfare.
1177 Beginning of a period when Angkor is captured by the Chams and then the Siamese.	
1432 Capital is moved to Phnom Penh region.	**1530** Beginning of transatlantic slave trade organized by the Portuguese in Africa
	1776 US Declaration of Independence
1863 Cambodia becomes a French protectorate.	
1866 Phnom Penh becomes the official capital.	**1869** The Suez Canal is opened.
1884 Cambodia becomes a French colony.	
1887 Cambodia becomes part of Indochina.	**1914** World War I begins.
	1939 World War II begins.
1941–1945 Cambodia is occupied by Japan during World War II.	**1945** The United States drops atomic bombs on Hiroshima and Nagasaki, Japan.
1953 Cambodia declares independence from France under King Sihanouk.	**1966–1969** The Chinese Cultural Revolution
1969 The United States begins bombing Cambodia.	
1970 Sihanouk takes refuge in Beijing, China.	
1975 Khmer Rouge occupies Cambodia, led by Pol Pot. Cambodia renamed Kampuchea.	

IN CAMBODIA	IN THE WORLD
1978	
Vietnam forces invade Cambodia and overthrow the Khmer Rouge.	**1986**
1989	Nuclear power disaster at Chernobyl in Ukraine
Vietnamese forces withdraw.	
1991	**1991**
Prince Sihanouk returns.	Breakup of the Soviet Union
1993	
General elections are held. Coalition government is formed between FUNCINPEC and Cambodian People's Party (CPP).	
1997	**1997**
Pol Pot is put on trial and sentenced to life imprisonment.	Hong Kong is returned to China.
1998	
Pol Pot dies.	
1999	
Cambodia joins ASEAN.	**2001**
2002	Terrorists crash planes in New York, Washington, DC, and Pennsylvania
First multiparty elections won by CPP; Hun Sen becomes prime minister.	**2003**
2004	War in Iraq begins.
Prime Minister Hun Sen is reelected; Cambodia enters World Trade Organization; King Sihanouk abdicates and is succeeded by his son, Norodom Sihamoni.	**2005**
	London hit by terrorist bombings
2008	**2008**
Cambodian and Thai soldiers exchange gunfire on the disputed border near Preah Vihar.	Barack Obama elected US president
2010	**2010**
The first conviction of a Khmer Rouge leader for crimes against humanity.	Massive earthquakes devastate Haiti and Chile.
2013–2014	
Protests over unfair elections and the low minimum wage take place.	**2015**
	The Paris Agreement on climate change is adopted.
2016	**2016**
Cambodia is reclassified as a lower-middle-income country instead of a low-income country by the World Bank.	The people of the United Kingdom vote to leave the European Union.

GLOSSARY

ansom chek (an-sam-KRU)
A rice-based dish made with tofu and pork, popular with Cambodians.

aspara (as-PAH-rah)
One of four motifs common in Khmer sculpture. They are mythical consorts of heavenly heroes and represent beauty in its ideal form.

chong roet (CHONG-rot)
Cicadas that are fried until crunchy—a favorite Cambodian delicacy.

chrieng (KRU-ng)
The angular form of the Khmer script in everyday use.

garuda (gah-ROO-dah)
Mythical half-man, half-bird creature found in Khmer architecture.

kaoet (COW-er)
Word, meaning "to be born," that is added to the number in the first half of a month.

muezzin (moo-EZ-in)
The mosque official who makes the call to prayer.

mul (MUL)
Rounded script of Khmer language used for special decorative purposes.

naga (nah-GAH)
Sacred snakes from Hindu mythology that act as guardians of water supplies.

nirvana (ner-VAH-na)
The final and perfect escape from karma that involves loss of individuality.

pong tea kon (PONG-tee-ko)
Duck eggs, which are eaten just before they are ready to hatch.

roc (raw)
A word, meaning "to grow less," that is added to the number in the second half of a month.

sangkcha khnor (SANK-cha kor)
Jackfruit pudding.

sarong (sah-RONG)
Loose garment worn by male and female Khmers and Chams, typically knotted at the waist.

sii bay (SEE-bay)
Cambodian verb meaning "to eat." Translated literally, it means "to eat rice."

singha (SING-ngah)
Mythical lions in Khmer architecture that act as guardians of temples.

tuk trey (TOUK-tra)
Fish sauce made by fermenting salted fish in large pots for three months or more.

wat (wat)
Temple.

FOR FURTHER INFORMATION

Books

Chandler, David. *A History of Cambodia*. Boulder, CO: Westview Press, 2009.

Ranges, Trevor. *National Geographic Traveler: Cambodia*. Washington, DC: National Geographic, 2010.

Saunders, Graham. *CultureShock! Cambodia: A Survival Guide to Customs and Etiquette*. London: Kuperard, 2008.

WEBSITES

Cambodian News. http://www.phnompenhpost.com

CIA *World Factbook*. http://www.cia.gov/cia/publications/factbook/geos/cb.html

Embassy of Cambodia in Washington, DC. http://www.embassyofcambodia.org

National Institute of Statistics. http://www.nis.gov.kh/index.php/en/

MUSIC

Cambodia: Folk and Ceremonial Music, UNESCO, 2014.

Cambodia: Royal Music, UNESCO, 2014.

Don't Think I've Forgotten: Cambodia's Lost Rock and Roll Soundtrack, Dust to Digital, 2015.

BIBLIOGRAPHY

Butler, Rhett. "Cambodia." *Mongabay*, August 15, 2014. http://rainforests.mongabay.com/20cambodia.htm.

Chandler, David P. *A History of Cambodia*. Boulder, CO: Westview Press, 2009.

———. *The Land and People of Cambodia*. New York, NY: Harper Collins, 1991.

Graff, Nancy Price. *Where the River Runs: A Portrait of a Refugee Family*. Boston, MA: Little, Brown, 1993.

Greenblatt, Miriam. *Cambodia*. Chicago, IL: Children's Press, 1995.

Ross, Russel, ed. *Cambodia: A Country Study*. Washington, DC: U.S. Government Printing Office, 1990.

Sam, Sien. *In the Land of the Red Prince*. New York, NY: Vantage Press, 1994.

The World Factbook. Washington, DC: Central Intelligence Agency. Retrieved August 1, 2015. https://www.cia.gov/library/publications/the-world-factbook/index.html.

Zsombor, Peter. "ADB Expects Cambodian Economy to Pick Up." *Cambodia Daily*, March 25, 2015. https://www.cambodiadaily.com/business/adb-expects-cambodian-economy-to-pick-up-80644.

INDEX

INDEX